Student Book

American Headway 2A

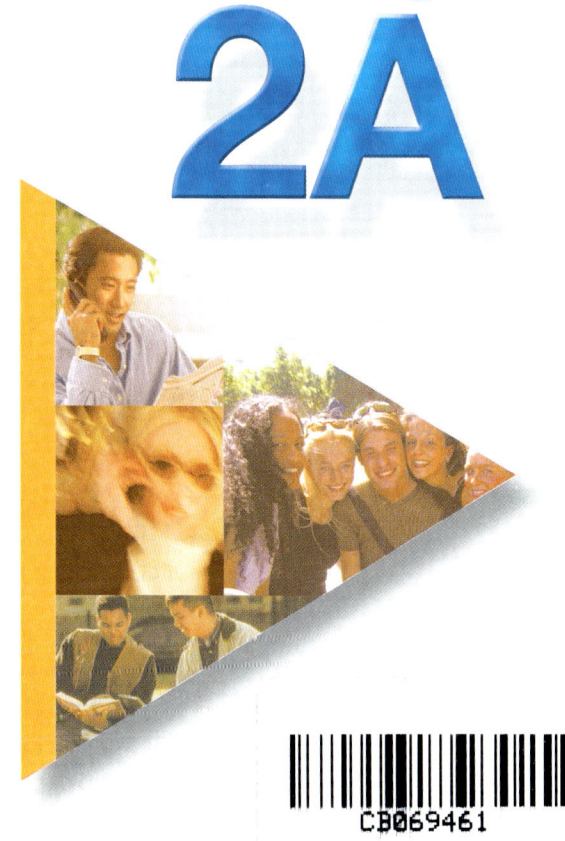

John and Liz Soars

OXFORD
UNIVERSITY PRESS

UNIVERSITY PRESS

198 Madison Avenue
New York, NY 10016 USA

Great Clarendon Street
Oxford OX2 6DP England

Oxford New York

Auckland Cape Town Dar es Salaam Hong Kong Karachi
Kuala Lumpur Madrid Melbourne Mexico City Nairobi
New Delhi Shanghai Taipei Toronto

With offices in

Argentina Austria Brazil Chile Czech Republic France Greece
Guatemala Hungary Italy Japan Poland Portugal Singapore
South Korea Switzerland Thailand Turkey Ukraine Vietnam

OXFORD is a trademark of Oxford University Press.

ISBN 978 0 19 437932 8

Copyright © 2001 Oxford University Press

The Library of Congress has cataloged the full edition as follows:

Soars, John
American headway. Student book 2 / John and Liz Soars.
   p. cm.
   1. English language–Textbooks for foreign speakers. 2. English language–United States–Problems, exercises, etc. 3. Americanisms–Problems, exercises, etc. I. Soars, Liz. II. Title.
PE 1128 .S5935 2001
428.2'4–dc21
                                                                 200132196

No unauthorized photocopying.

All rights reserved. No part of this publication may be reproduced, stored in a retrieval system, or transmitted, in any form or by any means, electronic, mechanical, photocopying, recording, or otherwise, without the prior written permission of Oxford University Press.

This book is sold subject to the condition that it shall not, by way of trade or otherwise, be lent, resold, hired out, or otherwise circulated without the publisher's prior consent in any form of binding or cover other than that in which it is published and without a similar condition including this condition being imposed on the subsequent purchaser.

American Headway Student Book 2A:
Editorial Manager: Shelagh Speers
Managing Editor: Jeff Krum
Editor: Pat O'Neill
Editorial Assistant: Alicia Dunn
Art Director: Lynn Luchetti
Designer: Shelley Himmelstein
Art Buyer/Picture Researcher: Laura Nash
Production Manager: Shanta Persaud
Production Coordinator: Eve Wong

Printing (last digit): 20 19 18 17 16 15 14 13 12 11

Printed in China.

Acknowledgments

Cover concept: Rowie Christopher
Cover design: Rowie Christopher and Silver Editions

Illustrations by Frank Bolle/Amcrican Artists Rep. Inc.; Carios Castellanos; Rowie Christopher; Ian Kellas; Gone Loco, Debut Art; Pierre Paul Pariseau; Andy Parker; Steve Pica; Harry Venning

Handwriting and realia by Susumu Kawabe

Location and studio photography by Gareth Boden, Dennis Kitchen, Mark Mason, Alexandre Militao, Stephen Ogilvy

The publishers would like to thank the following for their permission to reproduce photographs: L. Adamski Peek/Getty One Stone, M. Agliolo/Science Photo Library, Alaska Stock, F. Alison/Getty One Stone, The Ancient Art & Architecture Collection, AP, D. Armand/Getty One Stone, Guy Aroch/Corbis Outline, The Art Archive, B. Backman/Colorific!, Dave Bartruff/Corbis, C. Bernson/Colorific!, Bettmann/Corbis, Ed Bock/Corbis Stock Market, Michele Burgess/Corbis Stock Market, H. Camille/Getty One Stone, J. Carnemolla/Australian Picture Library, R. Chappie/Telegraph Colour Library, Jason Childs/FPG, Corbis, Corbis Stock Market, R.E. Daemrich/Getty One Stone, J. Danielsky/Telegraph Colour Library, F. Delva/Telegraph Colour Library, George B. Diebold/The Stock Market, Digital Vision, D. Ducros/Science Photo Library, Duomo/Corbis, C. Ehlers/Getty One Stone, K. Fisher/Getty One Stone, FPG, J.P. Fruchet/Telegraph Colour Library, R. Gage/Telegraph Colour Library, Getty News Services/MGM, Michael Goldman/FPG, T. Graham/Colorific!, Lauren Greenfield, L. Greenfield/Corbis Sygma, Sally & Richard Greenhill, John Henley/The Stock Market, R. Holmes/Corbis, M. Hutson/Redferns, Image Bank, J. Tove Johansson/Colorific!, Jordan/Frank Spooner Pictures, W. Kaehler/Getty One Stone, Michael Keller/Corbis Stock Market, R. La Salle/Getty One Stone, Lightscapes Inc./The Stock Market, D. Madison/Getty One Stone, Ryan McVay/PhotoDisc, Doug Menuez/PhotoDisc, S. Miller/Telegraph Colour Library, D. Modricker/COR/Corbis, L. Monneret/Getty One Stone, M. Mutor/Agencja Gazeta, I. O'Leary/Getty One Stone, C. Osborne/Corbis, Gregory Pace/Corbis/Sygma, PBJ Pictures/Getty One Stone, H. Pfeiffer/Getty One Stone, PhotoDisc, Picture Press/Corbis, Colin Raw/Stone, Reuters NewMedia Inc./Corbis, Robert Harding Picture Library, Martin Rogers/Stone, Rohan/Getty One Stone, M. Romanelli/The Image Bank, Ariel Skelly/Corbis Stock Market, Stone, Strauss/Curtis/Corbis Stock Market, Superstock, B. Thomas/Getty One Stone, Dan Tremain/PhotoDisc, Wartenberg/Picture Press/Corbis, LarryWilliams/Corbis Stock Market, Jeff Zaruba/The Stock Market

Special thanks to the Brooklyn Conservatory of Music

The publishers would also like to thank the following for their help:

p. 18 "The Burglar's Friend" The Daily Mail February 5,1996, © *The Daily Mail*/Solo Syndication. Used by permission.

p. 23 *The Man with the Golden Gun* by Jan Fleming Copyright © Glidrose Productions Ltd., 1965. Reproduced with the permission of Ian Fleming (Glidrose) Publications Ltd.

p. 31 "The Best Shopping Street in the World" by Anne Applebaum, *London Evening Standard* October 27, 1998, © *London Evening Standard*/Solo Syndication. Used by permission.

p. 40 "You've Got a Friend" Words and music by Carole King © 1971 COLGEMS-EMJ MUSIC INC. All Rights Reserved. International Copyright Secured. Used by Permission.

p. 47 "The Most Generous Man in the World" by Tony Burton, *Mail Weekend Magazine* December 31, 1994, © *Mail Weekend Magazine*/Solo Syndication. Used by permission.

Contents

	Scope and Sequence	iv
1	Getting to know you	2
2	The way we live	10
3	It all went wrong	18
4	Let's go shopping!	26
5	What do you want to do?	34
6	The best in the world	42
7	Fame	50
	Getting Information	114
	Tapescripts	128
	Grammar Reference	139
	Appendixes	153
	Phonetic Symbols	154

SCOPE AND SEQUENCE

Unit	Grammar	Vocabulary	Everyday English
1 Getting to know you page 2	**Tenses** Present, past, future pp. 2–4 **Questions** *Where were you born?* pp. 2–4 *What do you do?* **Question words** *Who … ?, Why … ?, How much … ?* p. 3	Using a bilingual dictionary p. 5 Parts of speech *adjective, preposition* p. 5 Words with more than one meaning *a book to read* *I booked a room at a hotel.* p. 5	Social expressions 1 *Have a good weekend!* *Same to you!* p. 9
2 The way we live page 10	**Present tenses** Present Simple *Most people live in the south.* p. 10 Present Continuous *What's she doing now?* p. 12 *have* *We have a population of …* p. 11 *Do you have a computer?* p. 12	Describing countries *a beautiful country* *the coast* *This country exports wool.* p. 10 Collocation Daily life *listen to music* *talk to my friends* p. 13	Making conversation Asking questions Showing that you're interested p. 17
3 It all went wrong page 18	**Past tenses** Past Simple *He heard a noise.* *What did you do last night?* p. 19 Past Continuous *A car was waiting.* p. 20	Irregular verbs *saw, went, told* p. 18 Making connections *break/fix, lose/find* p. 19 Nouns, verbs, and adjectives Suffixes to make different parts of speech *discuss, discussion* p. 24 Making negatives *pack, unpack* p. 24	Time expressions *January eighth* *at six o'clock* *on Saturday* *in 1995* p. 25
4 Let's go shopping! page 26	**Quantity** *much* and *many* *How much milk? How many eggs?* p. 26 *some* and *any* *some apples, any grapes* p. 27 *something, anyone, nobody, everywhere* p. 28 *a few, a little, a lot of* p. 27 **Articles** *a general store, a small town, the army* *He sells bread.* p. 29	Buying things *milk, eggs, bread, a jar of jam,* *a can of soda, shampoo, soap,* *sweaters, department store,* *antique store, newsstand, sneakers,* *a tie, conditioner, first-class stamps*	Prices and shopping *£1.99* *$16.40* *What's the exchange rate?* *How much is a pair of jeans?* p. 33
5 What do you want to do? page 34	**Verb patterns 1** *want/hope to do, enjoy/like doing* *looking forward to doing, 'd like to do* p. 34 **Future intentions** *going to* and *will* *She's going to travel around the world.* *I'll pick it up for you.* p. 36	Hot verbs *have, go, come* *have an accident* *go wrong* *come in first* p. 40	How do you feel? *nervous, excited* *Cheer up!* p. 41
6 The best in the world page 42	**What's it like?** *What's Paris like?* p. 42 **Comparative and superlative adjectives** *big, bigger, biggest* *good, better, best* p. 43	Talking about cities *modern buildings, nightlife* p. 43 Money *make money, inherit* p. 46 Synonyms and antonyms *nice, beautiful, interested, bored* p. 48	Directions *park, woods, pond* *across from the flower shop* *over the bridge* p. 49
7 Fame page 50	**Present Perfect and Past Simple** *She has made over 17 albums.* *He recorded 600 songs.* p. 50 *for* and *since* *for three years* *since 1989* p. 52 **Tense review** *Where do you live?* *How long have you lived there?* *Why did you move?* p. 52	Past participles *lived, sang* p. 50 Bands and music *guitar, keyboards* *make a record* p. 53 Adverbs *slowly, carefully, just, still, too* p. 56 Word pairs *now and then* *ladies and gentlemen* p. 56	Short answers *Do you like cooking?* *Yes, I do.* *No, I don't.* p. 57

Reading	Speaking	Listening	Writing (in the Workbook)
"People, the great communicators"—the many ways we communicate p. 7	Information gap—Judy Dandridge p. 4 Discussion—who are your ideal neighbors? p. 8 Role play—exchanging information about two neighbors p. 8	Neighbors—Steve and Mrs. Snell talk about each other as neighbors (jigsaw) p. 8	Informal letters A letter to a pen pal WB p. 5
"Living in the USA"—three people talk about their experiences (jigsaw) p. 14	Information gap—people's lifestyles p. 12 Exchanging information about immigrants to the USA p. 14	"You drive me crazy (but I love you)!"—what annoys you about the people in your life? p. 16	Linking words *but, however, so, because* WB p. 10 Describing a person WB p. 11
"The burglars' friend" p. 18 Newspaper stories p. 20 A spy story—"The Man with the Golden Gun" p. 23	Information gap—Sue's party p. 21 Telling stories *fortunately/unfortunately* p. 21	A spy story—"The Man with the Golden Gun" p. 22	Linking words *while, during,* and *for* WB p. 16 Writing a story 1 WB p. 17
"The best shopping street in the world"—Nowy Swiat, in Poland p. 30	Town survey—the good things and bad things about living in your town p. 28 Discussion—attitudes to shopping p. 30	"The happiest man I know" p. 29 Buying things p. 32	Filling out forms WB p. 22
"Hollywood kids—What's it like when you have it all?" p. 38	What are your plans and ambitions? p. 35 Being a teenager p. 38	A song—"You've Got a Friend" p. 40	Writing a postcard WB p. 28
"A tale of two millionaires"—one was stingy and one was generous p. 46	Information gap—comparing cities p. 44 Discussion—the rich and their money p. 46	Living in another country—an interview with a woman who went to live in Sweden p. 45	Relative clauses 1 *who/that/which/where* WB p. 33 Describing a place WB p. 33
Celebrity interview from *Hi! Magazine* with the pop star and the baseball player who are in love p. 54	Mingle—Find someone who … p. 51 Role play—interviewing a band p. 53 Project—find an interview with a famous person p. 54	An interview with the band Style p. 53	Relative clauses 2 *who/which/that* as the object WB p. 37 Writing a biography WB p. 38

1 Getting to know you

Tenses • Questions • Using a bilingual dictionary • Social expressions 1

STARTER

1 Match the questions and answers.

Where were you born?	A year ago.
What do you do?	Three times a week.
Are you married?	In Thailand.
Why are you studying English?	Because I need it for my job.
When did you start learning English?	I'm a teacher.
How often do you have English classes?	No, I'm single.

2 Ask and answer the questions with a partner.

TWO STUDENTS
Tenses and questions

1 **T 1.1** Read and listen to Mauricio. Then complete the text using the verbs in the box.

| 'm enjoying | 'm going to work | live | started |
| 'm studying | come | can speak | went |

My name's **Mauricio Nesta**. I (1) __come__ from Brasilia, the capital of Brazil. I'm a student at the University of Brasilia. I (2) _____ modern languages—English and French. I also know a little Spanish, so I (3) _____ four languages. I (4) _____ the program a lot, but it's really hard work. I (5) _____ college three years ago.

I (6) _____ at home with my parents and my sister. My brother (7) _____ to work in the United States last year.

After I graduate, I (8) _____ as a translator. I hope so, anyway.

2 Unit 1 • Getting to know you

2 Complete the questions about Carly.

1. _Where does she_ come from?
   _____
2. _____ live?
   _____
3. _____ live with?
   _____
4. What _____ studying?
   _____
5. _____ enjoying the program?
   _____
6. How many _____ speak?
   _____
7. _____ did her program start?
   _____
8. What _____ after she graduates?
   _____

T 1.2 Listen to Carly, and write the answers to the questions above.

3 Carly is also a student. Read her answers, then complete the questions.

1. "What _university do you go_ to?"
   "I don't go to a university. I study at home."
2. "_____ a job?"
   "Yes, I do. A part-time job."
3. "What _____ right now?"
   "I'm reading about Italian art."
4. "_____ to the United States?"
   "Fifteen years ago."
5. "_____ name?"
   "Dave."
6. "_____?"
   "He's an architect."

Carly Robson

GRAMMAR SPOT

1 Find examples of present, past, and future tenses in Exercises 1 and 2 above.
2 Which tenses are the two verb forms in these sentences? What is the difference between them?
   He lives with his parents.
   She's living with a Canadian family for a month.
3 Match the question words and answers.

What … ?	Because I wanted to.
Who … ?	Last night.
Where … ?	$5.00.
When … ?	A sandwich.
Why … ?	By bus.
How many … ?	In Miami.
How much … ?	Jack.
How … ?	The black one.
Whose … ?	It's mine.
Which … ?	Four.

▶▶ Grammar Reference 1.1 and 1.2 p. 139

Unit 1 • Getting to know you

PRACTICE

Talking about you

1 Ask and answer questions with a partner.
- Where ... live?
- ... have any brothers or sisters?
- What ... like doing on weekends?
- Where ... go for your last vacation?

Make more questions. Use some of the question words in the Grammar Spot on page 3. Ask your teacher some of the questions.

2 In groups, ask and answer the questions.
- Do you like listening to music?
- What kind of music do you like?
- What are you wearing?
- What is your teacher wearing?
- What did you do last night?
- What are you doing tonight?

3 Write a paragraph about you. Use the text about Mauricio on page 2 to help you.

Getting information

4 Work with a partner.

You each have different information about Judy Dandridge, a mail carrier. Ask and answer questions.

Student A Go to page 114.
Student B Go to page 116.

Check it

5 Choose the correct verb form.
1. Maria *comes* / *is coming* from Chile.
2. She *speaks* / *is speaking* Spanish and English.
3. Today Tom *wears* / *is wearing* jeans and a T-shirt.
4. *Are you liking* / *Do you like* black coffee?
5. Last year she *went* / *goes* on vacation to Florida.
6. Next year she *studies* / *is going to study* at a university in California.

4 Unit 1 · Getting to know you

VOCABULARY
Using a bilingual dictionary

1 Look at this extract from the *Oxford Portuguese Minidictionary*.

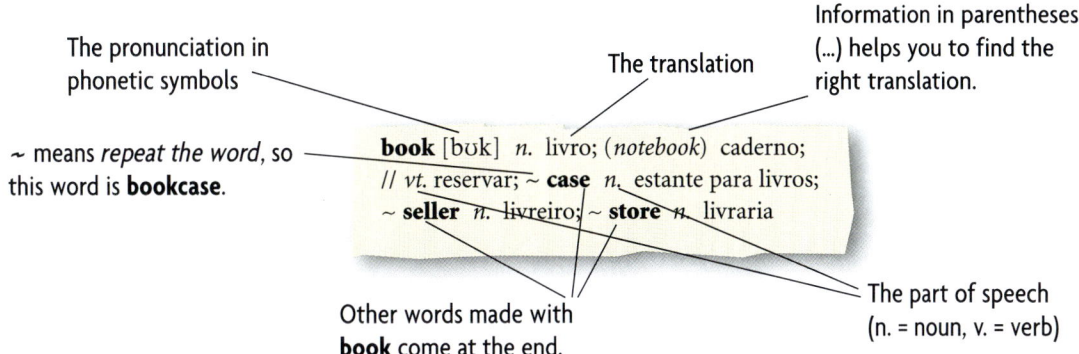

The pronunciation in phonetic symbols

The translation

Information in parentheses (...) helps you to find the right translation.

~ means *repeat the word*, so this word is **bookcase**.

Other words made with **book** come at the end.

The part of speech (n. = noun, v. = verb)

2 What parts of speech are these words? Write *noun*, *verb*, *adjective*, *adverb*, *preposition*, or *past tense verb*.

bread	**noun**	beautiful	_____	on	_____
funny	_____	in	_____	came	_____
write	_____	never	_____	eat	_____
quickly	_____	went	_____	letter	_____

3 These words have more than one meaning. Write two sentences that show different meanings. Use a dictionary.

	Sentence 1	**Sentence 2**
1. book	I'm reading a good book.	I booked a room at a hotel.
2. kind		
3. can		
4. mean		
5. light		
6. play		
7. train		
8. ring		

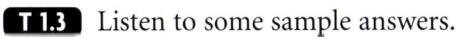 Listen to some sample answers.

4 What are the everyday objects in the pictures? Look around the room you are in. Find five things you don't know the words for in English. Look them up in a dictionary.

READING
Communication

1 How many different ways can people communicate?

2 Work with a partner. You will get some ideas to communicate, but you can't use words. Mime the ideas.
   Student A Go to page 118.
   Student B Go to page 120.

3 Read the text on page 7 quickly and match the correct heading to each paragraph.

A **HISTORY** OF COMMUNICATION

HOW WE COMMUNICATE

COMMUNICATION **TODAY**

DIFFERENCES BETWEEN **PEOPLE** AND **ANIMALS**

4 Read the text again and answer the questions.
   1. Which animals are mentioned? What can they do?
   2. What is special about human communication? What can *we* do?
   3. Which four forms of media are mentioned in the last paragraph?
   4. What is good and bad about information technology today?

What do you think?

- What can animals do that people can't?
- How do *you* like to communicate?
- What is happening in information technology now?

PEOPLE
THE GREAT COMMUNICATORS

We can communicate with other people in many different ways. We can talk and write, and we can send messages with our hands and faces. There is also the telephone (including the cell phone!), the fax, and e-mail. Television, movies, painting, and photography can also communicate ideas.

Animals have ways of exchanging information, too. Bees dance and tell other bees where to find food. Elephants make sounds that humans can't hear. Whales sing songs. Monkeys use their faces to show anger and love. But this is nothing compared to what people can do. We have language—about 6,000 languages, in fact. We can write poetry, tell jokes, make promises, explain, persuade, tell the truth, or tell lies. And we have a sense of past and future, not just present.

Communication technologies were very important in the development of ancient societies:
- Around 2900 B.C., paper and hieroglyphics transformed Egyptian life.
- The ancient Greeks loved the spoken word. They were very good at public speaking, drama, and philosophy.
- The Romans developed a unique system of government that depended on the Roman alphabet.
- In the fifteenth century, the printing press helped develop new ways of thinking across Europe.

Radio, movies, and television have had a huge influence on society in the last hundred years. And now we have the Internet, which is infinite. But what is this doing to us? We can give and get a lot of information very quickly. But there is so much information that it is difficult to know what is important and what isn't. Modern media are changing our world every minute of every day.

LISTENING AND SPEAKING
Neighbors

1. What are your ideal neighbors like? Complete the questionnaire on the right, then discuss your answers with a partner.

2. "Good fences make good neighbors." What does this mean? Do you agree?

3. You will hear Mrs. Snell and her new neighbor, Steve, talking about each other.

    Work in two groups.

    T 1.4 **Group A** Listen to Mrs. Snell.

    T 1.5 **Group B** Listen to Steve.

4. Answer the questions.
    1. When did Steve move into his new apartment?
    2. Is it a big apartment?
    3. Who is staying with Steve at the moment?
    4. Where does he work?
    5. Does he work long hours?
    6. What does he wear to work?
    7. How many people came to the party?
    8. What time did Steve's party end?
    9. What is Steve doing tonight?

    Compare your answers with a partner from the other group. What are the differences?

Role play

Work in groups of three.

Student A You are Steve.
Student B You are Mrs. Snell.
Student C You are another neighbor. You have invited Steve and Mrs. Snell to your apartment for coffee.

Make polite conversation. Talk about these things:
- Steve's job
- Steve's sister
- Steve's party

Neighbor	Do you two know each other?
Steve	Well, no. Not really.
Mrs. Snell	No.
Neighbor	Mrs. Snell, this is Steve James, our new neighbor. Steve, this is Mrs. Snell.
Steve	Nice to meet you, Mrs. Snell.
Mrs. Snell	Nice to meet you, Steve.
Neighbor	Steve works in advertising, you know ...

What do you think?

Write down three things that young people think about older people and three things that older people think about young people. In groups, compare ideas.

QUESTIONNAIRE

My ideal neighbors are people who ...

	Yes	No
... say hello when I see them.	☐	☐
... I never see.	☐	☐
... have parties and invite me.	☐	☐
... are very quiet.	☐	☐
... often come over for a cup of coffee.	☐	☐
... come over to borrow things.	☐	☐
... make themselves at home in my house.	☐	☐

EVERYDAY ENGLISH
Social expressions 1

1 We use certain expressions in different social situations.

> *I'm sorry I'm late!*

> *That's OK. Come in and sit down.*

Match the expressions and responses. When do we use these expressions?

1. How are you?	Sleep well!
2. Hello, Jane!	Yes. Can I help you?
3. See you tomorrow!	Good morning!
4. Good night!	Fine, thanks.
5. Good morning!	Nice to meet you, Elaine.
6. Hello, I'm Elaine Paul.	You're welcome.
7. Cheers!	Thanks.
8. Excuse me.	Same to you!
9. Make yourself at home.	Cheers!
10. Have a good weekend!	Bye! See you then.
11. Thank you very much.	Hi, Peter!
12. Bless you!	Thank you. That's very nice of you.

T 1.6 Listen and check. Practice saying the expressions.

2 Test a partner. Say an expression. Can your partner give the correct response?

3 With your partner, write two short conversations that include some of the social expressions. Read your conversations to the class.

Unit 1 · Getting to know you 9

2 The way we live

Present tenses • *have* • Collocation — daily life • Making conversation

STARTER Match the flags with the countries they belong to. They are all English-speaking countries.

1. Australia

3. _____

5. _____

2. _____

4. _____

6. _____

the United States
Canada
Australia
New Zealand
South Africa
the United Kingdom

PEOPLE AND PLACES
Present tenses

1 Complete each text with the words in the box. Then match a country from the Starter and a photograph to each text.

a ☐ exports enjoy immigrants huge

This country has a fairly small population, just 16 million, but its area is _huge_ . The people are mainly of European descent, but there are also aborigines and a lot of southeast Asian ____ . People live in towns on the coast, not so much inland, because it is so hot. They live a lot of their lives outdoors, and ____ sports, swimming, and having barbecues. This country ____ wine and wool—it has more than 60 million sheep!

b ☐ popular variety has only

This is the second biggest country in the world, but it has a population of ____ 30 million. It is so big that there is a ____ of climates. Most people live in the south because the north is too cold. It is famous for its beautiful mountains and lakes—it ____ more lakes than any other country. Two of the most ____ sports are ice hockey and baseball.

c ☐ elephants grows black climate

This country has a population of about 45 million. Of these, 76 percent are ____ and 12 percent white. It has a warm ____ . Either it never rains, or it rains a lot! It is the world's biggest producer of gold, and it exports diamonds, too. It ____ a lot of fruit, including oranges, pears, and grapes, and it makes wine. In the game reserves you can see a lot of wildlife, including lions, ____ , zebras, and giraffes.

10 Unit 2 • The way we live

2 **T 2.1** Listen to three people describing the other countries. Match a country and photograph with each description.

 d   e   f

3 Close your books. Can you remember three facts about each country? Tell a partner.

4 Give some similar facts about your country.

GRAMMAR SPOT

1 What tense are all the verb forms in texts *a–c*? Why?
2 Look at the sentences. Which refers to *all the time*? Which refers to *right now*?
   She has three children.
   She's having lunch.

▶▶ Grammar Reference 2.1 p. 140

Unit 2 • The way we live   11

PRACTICE

Talking about you

1 Practice the forms of the Present Simple in the question, short answer, and negative.

1. have a computer/a car
2. your father work in an office?

Do you have a computer?

Yes, I do.

Do you have a car?

No, I don't. I just have a bicycle.

Does your father work in an office?

No, he doesn't. He works in a school. He's a teacher ...

T 2.2 Listen and repeat.

2 Ask and answer questions about these things with a partner.
- have a cell phone/a credit card/a pet?
- sometimes wear jeans/sneakers/a hat?
- drink tea/coffee/wine?
- your family live in an apartment?
- your grandmother live near you?
- your sister/brother have a boyfriend/girlfriend?

Tell the class some things about your partner.

Roberto has a cell phone, but he doesn't have a computer. He ...

3 Practice the Present Continuous. What are you doing now? What is your teacher doing?

Are you ...	Is she/he ...		
... sitting down?	... standing up?	... talking?	... writing?
... smiling?	... laughing?	... working hard?	

Talk to your partner.

I'm sitting down and I'm working very hard. My teacher's laughing!

4 Write questions to find the information about the people on the right.

City/country	• Where does he ... from?
Family	• ... she married?
	• ... they have any ... ?
	• How many brothers and sisters ... she ... ?
Occupation	• What ... he do?
Free time/vacation	• What ... she ... in her free time?
	• Where ... they go on vacation?
Current activity	• What ... she doing right now?

T 2.3 Listen and check.

Getting information

5 Work with a partner.

Student A Go to page 115.
Student B Go to page 117.

Unit 2 • The way we live

6 Think of questions to ask about free time and vacation activities.

- What do you do in your free time?
- What do ... on weekends?
- ... any sports?
- Do you ... any hobbies?
- Do you like ... ?
- Where ... vacation?

Stand up! Ask three students your questions. Use short answers when necessary. Find out who has the most hobbies and best vacations.

Do you like skiing?   *No, I don't.*

Check it

7 Put a check (✓) next to the correct sentence.

1. ☐ Where you go on vacation?
   ☐ Where do you go on vacation?
2. ☐ I'm Yaling. I'm coming from Taiwan.
   ☐ I'm Yaling. I come from Taiwan.
3. ☐ This is a great party! Everyone is dancing.
   ☐ This is a great party! Everyone dances.
4. ☐ I don't have a cell phone.
   ☐ I no have a cell phone.
5. ☐ Jack's a police officer, but he doesn't wear a uniform.
   ☐ Jack's a police officer, but he no wear a uniform.
6. ☐ "Where is Pete?" "He's sitting by the window."
   ☐ "Where is Pete?" "He sits by the window."
7. ☐ I'm liking black coffee.
   ☐ I like black coffee.

VOCABULARY
Daily life

1 Match the verbs and nouns.

have	a movie on TV
wash	to my friends
watch	my hair
talk	breakfast

make	to music
listen	my homework
relax	some coffee
do	on the sofa

take	posters on the wall
clean up	the mess
do	a shower
have/put	the dishes

cook	magazines
go	a meal
put on	makeup
read	to the bathroom

T 2.4 Listen and check.

2 Match the activities from Exercise 1 with the correct room.

Kitchen
_____
_____
_____
_____

Bathroom
_____
_____
_____
_____

Living room
_____
_____
_____
_____

Bedroom
_____
_____
_____
_____

3 Do you like where you live? Choose your favorite room. What do you do in that room?

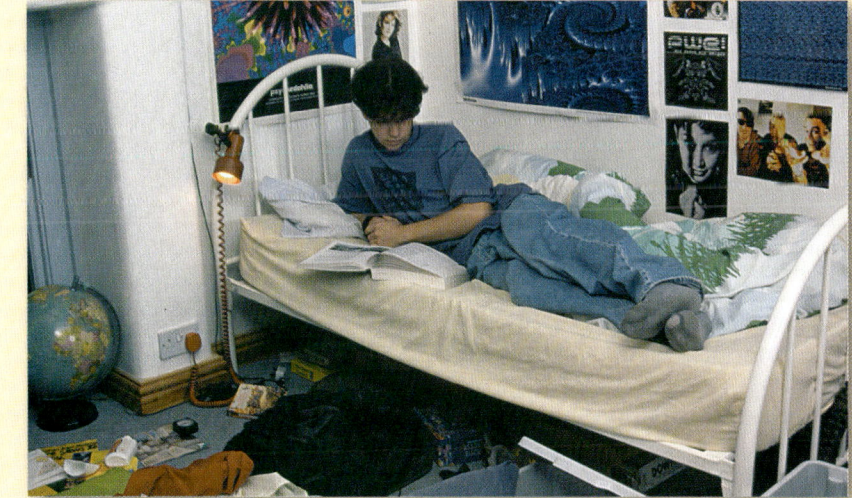

I like my bedroom a lot because I have lots of posters on the walls. I listen to music and do my homework ...

I like my living room. The walls are white, and I love the big, comfortable sofa ...

4 Describe your favorite room to a partner. Don't say which room it is. Can your partner guess?

READING AND SPEAKING
Living in the USA

1. Close your eyes and think of the United States. Write down the first five things you think of.

   The Empire State Building
   Cheeseburgers and fries

   Compare your list with other students.

2. Read the introduction to the magazine article. Then work in three groups.

   Group A Read about Roberto.
   Group B Read about Endre.
   Group C Read about Yuet.

3. Answer the questions.
   1. Why and when did he/she come to the United States?
   2. What does he/she do?
   3. What does he/she like about living in the United States?
   4. What was difficult at the beginning?

4. Find a partner from each of the other two groups. Compare the three people.

5. Answer the questions with your group.
   1. What do the people have in common?
   2. Are they all happy living in the United States?
   3. Who has other members of their family living in the United States?
   4. Do they all have children?
   5. Who married someone from their own country?
   6. What do Roberto and Endre like about the United States?
   7. What do they say about their own country?
   8. Do they like the people in the United States?
   9. What do they say about Americans and their cars?

What do you think?

- What do you like best about living in your country? What would you miss if you lived abroad?
- Do you know any foreigners living in your country? What do they like about it? What do they say is different?

14 Unit 2 • The way we live

LIVING IN

Every year, tens of thousands of people from around the world travel to the United States to study or visit. But what is it like to live there? How do people like the US when they first arrive? What do they think of the people and the way of life?

Jeff Peterson spoke to three people.

THE USA

Roberto Solano
from Mexico

Endre Boros
from Hungary

Yuet Tung
from Hong Kong

Roberto came from Mexico to New York ten years ago. At first he missed everything—the sunshine, the food, his girlfriend. But now he has a successful business with his three brothers and his sister. They run a soccer store in a small town near New York City. Roberto's girlfriend is now his wife, and they have two children.

When asked why he came to the United States, Roberto says without hesitation, "Because I want to work hard and have my own business." He certainly works hard. He's at the store all day, then works as a driver in the evening. "That's why I like America," he says. "You can be whatever you want."

"When I first came here, I only spoke Spanish. Then I went to high school and learned English. The people were friendly, but I missed my family. Now nearly all my family are here. We meet about once a month and have a huge Mexican meal that takes about five hours! We're all happy here."

Endre is a professor at Rutgers University in New Jersey. He came from Budapest 13 years ago. "I had an opportunity to come here for two years." After a year, his wife came to join him, and since then they've had a daughter, so they decided to stay.

"At first it was very strange. Everything is so big here," he says. "I started to feel happy when I bought a car. Now I go everywhere by car. In Hungary, we only use the car on weekends, but here your car is part of your life. Nobody walks anywhere."

What does he think of the people? "Very friendly. The first question everybody asks you is 'Where are you from?' People talk to you here, they start conversations."

What about the way of life? "The thing I like best is the independence. Nobody tells me what to do. Here you can do what you want, so you learn to make decisions for yourself. I feel in control."

Yuet is her Chinese name, but in English she's known as Clara. She came to the United States eight years ago and studied fine art. Now she works on Madison Avenue for a publishing company. She married a Vietnamese American three years ago, and they live in a suburb of New York. They don't have any children yet.

How does she like working in New York? "It's very similar to Hong Kong. It's a busy city, very exciting, and people walk very fast! I like the stores here. They're huge, and it's cheaper than Hong Kong. In Hong Kong everyone uses public transportation because it's good and it's cheap. But you need a car here. At first I hated driving, but it's OK now."

What does she like best? "The space. Here I live in a house with a yard. In Hong Kong it is so crowded. And the people here are friendly. When I go jogging, everyone says 'Hi!' And the food is from every country in the world."

Unit 2 • The way we live 15

LISTENING AND SPEAKING
You drive me crazy (but I love you)!

1 Complete these sentences about the people in your life. Tell a partner.
   - My mother/father drives me crazy when she/he ...
   - I hate it when my boyfriend/girlfriend ...
   - I don't like friends who ...
   - It really annoys me when people ...

2 Choose one person in your life. What annoying habits does he/she have?

   Does he/she ... ?
   - always arrive late
   - talk too loudly
   - leave things on the floor

   Is he/she ... ?
   - messy
   - always on the phone
   - never on time

   What annoying habits do *you* have? Discuss with your partner.

3 You are going to listen to a radio program called *Home Truths*. Two couples, Carol and Mike, and Dave and Alison, talk about their partner's annoying habits. Look at the pictures below. What are their annoying habits?

   T 2.5 Listen and write the correct name under each picture below.

1 Alison

3

5

7

2

4

6

8

4 Are these sentences true (✓) or false (✗)? Correct the false sentences.
   1. Carol and Mike never watch television.
   2. Mike doesn't listen when his wife speaks to him.
   3. Carol makes the decisions in their house.
   4. Mike asks his wife for directions whenever he's driving.
   5. Dave never does any jobs at home.
   6. Dave is bad at his job.
   7. Dave is very messy.
   8. Alison is usually on time.

What do you think?

1 Do men or women typically complain about their partners doing these things?
   - watching sports on TV
   - telling the other how to drive
   - taking a long time to get ready
   - being messy

2 What do you think men are generally better at? What are women better at?

EVERYDAY ENGLISH
Making conversation

1 **T 2.6** Listen to two conversations. Maria and Sergio are foreign students in the United States. Their teachers are trying to be friendly. Which conversation is more successful? Why?

2 Obviously, it is impossible to tell someone how to have a conversation, but here are some things that help.
- Ask questions.
- Show that you're interested.
- Don't just answer *yes* or *no*.
- Try to add a comment of your own.
- Don't let the conversation stop.

Find examples of these points in the tapescript on page 129.

3 Match a line in **A** with a reply in **B** and a further comment in **C**.

A	B	C
1. What a nice day it is today!	I'm enjoying it.	What was the score?
2. How are you today?	Yes, no problems.	We went to the beach and did some shopping.
3. Did you have a nice weekend?	Fine, thanks.	The plane was a little late, but it didn't matter.
4. How do you like living in Texas?	No, I missed it.	I got it in San Francisco last year.
5. Did you have a good flight?	Thank you.	How about you?
6. Did you watch the soccer game yesterday?	Yes.	It was kind of strange at first, but I'm getting used to it.
7. What a beautiful coat you're wearing!	Yes, we had a great time.	It's beautiful, isn't it?

T 2.7 Listen and check. Practice the conversations with a partner.

4 Think of three questions to ask someone about each of these subjects.
- job • home • free time • last vacation

5 Invent a new name and background for yourself.

> *My name's James Bond. I'm a spy. I have homes in London, Moscow, and Beijing ...*

Stand up! You're all at a party. Try to make some friends.

3 It all went wrong

Past tenses • Word formation • Time expressions

STARTER Here are the past tense forms of some irregular verbs. Write the present tenses.

1. _are_ were
2. _____ saw
3. _____ went
4. _____ told
5. _____ said
6. _____ had
7. _____ took
8. _____ gave
9. _____ got
10. _____ could
11. _____ made
12. _____ did

THE BURGLARS' FRIEND
Past Simple

1 Read and listen to the newspaper article. Why was Russell the burglars' friend?

The Burglars' Friend

IT WAS 3 O'CLOCK IN THE morning when four-year-old Russell Brown woke up to go to the bathroom.

His parents were fast asleep in bed. But when he heard a noise in the living room and saw a light was on, he went downstairs.

There he found two men. They asked him his name and told him they were friends of the family.

Unfortunately, Russell believed them. They asked him where the VCR and TV were. Russell showed them and said they had a stereo and CD player, too.

The two men carried these to the kitchen. Russell also told them that his mother kept her wallet in a drawer in the kitchen, so they took that. Russell even gave them his pocket money—50 cents.

They finally left at 4 A.M. They said, "Will you open the back door while we take these things to the car, because we don't want to wake Mommy and Daddy, OK?" So Russell held the door open for them. He then went back to bed.

His parents didn't know about the burglary until they got up the next day. His father said, "I couldn't be angry with Russell because he thought he was doing the right thing."

Fortunately, the police caught the two burglars last week.

18 Unit 3 • It all went wrong

2 Write the past forms of these irregular verbs from the article.

wake	_woke_	leave	_____
hear	_____	hold	_____
find	_____	think	_____
keep	_____	catch	_____

3 **T 3.2** You will hear some sentences about the story. Correct the mistakes.

Russell woke up at 2 o'clock.

> He didn't wake up at 2:00! He woke up at 3:00.

4 Write the questions to these answers.
1. Because he wanted to go to the bathroom.
   Why did he wake up?
2. They were in bed.
3. Because he heard a noise and saw a light on.
4. Two.
5. They told him they were friends of the family.
6. In a drawer in the kitchen.
7. Fifty cents.
8. At 4 A.M.
9. The next day. *(When … find out about … ?)*
10. Last week.

Russell, 4, made thieves feel at home

GRAMMAR SPOT

1 What tense are nearly all the verbs in the article? Why? How do we form the question and negative?

2 Write the Past Simple of these verbs.

a. ask	_asked_	c. like	_____
show	_____	believe	_____
want	_____	use	_____
walk	_____		
start	_____		
b. try	_____	d. stop	_____
carry	_____	plan	_____

T 3.3 Listen and repeat.

3 How is the regular past tense formed?
How is the past tense formed when the verb ends in a consonant + *y*?
When do we double the final consonant?

There is a list of irregular verbs on page 153.

▶▶ Grammar Reference 3.1 p. 141

PRACTICE

Making connections

1 Match the verb phrases. Then make sentences using both verbs in the past. Join the sentences with *so, because, and,* or *but.*

I broke a cup, but I fixed it with glue.

1. break a cup	answer it
2. feel sick	fix it
3. make a sandwich	wash my hair
4. take a shower	laugh
5. lose my passport	be hungry
6. call the police	go to bed
7. run out of coffee	buy some more
8. forget her birthday	find it
9. phone ring	say I was sorry
10. tell a joke	hear a strange noise

T 3.4 Listen and compare your answers.

Talking about you

2 Ask and answer these questions with a partner. Make more questions using the Past Simple.

What did you do … ?
- last night
- last weekend
- on your last birthday
- on your last vacation

> *I watched TV.*

> *I went swimming.*

NEWSPAPER STORIES
Past Continuous

1 Read each text and <u>underline</u> the Past Simple of the verbs in the boxes.

| have   can   steal   give   say |

| break   hear   come   leave   go |

a
Hands up, I've got a burger!

Last Tuesday a man armed with just a hot hamburger in a bag <u>stole</u> $1,000 from a bank in Danville, California. Police Detective Bill McGinnis said that the robber (1) _____ , entered the Mount Diablo National Bank at about 1:30 P.M. and gave the teller a note demanding $1,000. He claimed that he had a bomb in the bag. The teller said she could smell a distinct odor of hamburger coming from the bag. Even so, she handed the money to the man. (2) _____ , he dropped the bag with the hamburger. He escaped in a car (3) _____ .

Police Detective Bill McGinnis

b
Teenage party ends in tears

When Jack and Kelly Harman went away on vacation, they left their teenage daughter alone in the house. Sue, aged 16, wanted to stay at home (4) _____ . Her parents said she could have some friends stay over. However, Sue decided to have a party. (5) _____ things started to go wrong. Forty uninvited guests arrived (6) _____ . They broke furniture, smashed windows, and stole jewelry. When Mr. and Mrs. Harman heard the news, they came home immediately.

Sue Harman, 16, home alone

2 Match each phrase to an article. Where exactly does each phrase go?

- because she was studying for a test
- as he was running out of the bank
- everyone was having a good time when suddenly
- that was waiting for him outside
- and some of them were carrying knives
- who was wearing a mask

T 3.5 Listen and check. Practice the sentences.

GRAMMAR SPOT

1. The verb forms in Exercise 2 are in the Past Continuous. Complete the forms of the Past Continuous.

   I <u>was studying</u>.   We _____ waiting.
   You _____ studying.   They _____ waiting.
   She _____ studying.

2. Look at these sentences. What's the difference between them?

   When we arrived, | she made / she was making | some coffee.

▶▶ Grammar Reference 3.2 and 3.3 p. 142

20 Unit 3 • It all went wrong

PRACTICE

Discussing grammar

1 Choose the correct verb form.
   1. I *saw* / *was seeing* a very good program on TV last night.
   2. While I *shopped* / *was shopping* this morning, I *lost* / *was losing* my wallet. I don't know how.
   3. Last week the police *stopped* / *were stopping* Alan in his car because he *drove* / *was driving* at over 120 kilometers an hour.
   4. How *did you cut* / *were you cutting* your finger?
   5. I *cooked* / *was cooking* and I *dropped* / *was dropping* the knife.
   6. When I *arrived* / *was arriving* at the party, everyone *had* / *was having* a good time.
   7. *Did you have* / *Were you having* a good time on your vacation last month?

2 Complete the sentences with the verbs in the Past Simple or Past Continuous.
   1. While I **was going** (go) to work this morning, I _____ (meet) an old friend.
   2. I _____ (not want) to get up this morning. It _____ (rain) and it was cold, and my bed was so warm.
   3. I _____ (listen) to the news on the radio when the phone _____ (ring).
   4. But when I _____ (pick) up the phone, there was no one there.
   5. I _____ (say) "Hello" to the children, but they didn't say anything because they _____ (watch) television.

Getting information

3 Work with a partner. You will each have information about the teenage party, but you don't have all the information. Ask and answer questions.

   Student A Go to page 118.
   Student B Go to page 120.

fortunately/unfortunately

4 Continue this story around the class.

I went out for a walk.
Unfortunately, it began to rain.
Fortunately, I had an umbrella.
Unfortunately, it was broken.
Fortunately, I met a friend in his car.
Unfortunately, his car ran out of gas.
Fortunately, …

5 Tell similar stories around the class. Begin with these sentences.
   - I lost my wallet yesterday.
   - It was my birthday last week.
   - We went out for dinner last night.
   - I went on vacation to … last year.

LISTENING AND READING
A spy story

1 Who is James Bond? Write down anything you know about him and share ideas with the class.

2 The following are titles of James Bond movies. Have you seen any of these movies?

| Goldfinger |
| From Russia with Love |
| The Man with the Golden Gun |
| The Spy Who Loved Me |
| GoldenEye |
| Tomorrow Never Dies |

Do you know any more James Bond movies?

Do you know the translation of any of the titles in your language?

3 **T 3.6** You are going to listen to an extract from *The Man with the Golden Gun*. Cover the story on page 23 and look at the pictures. What can you guess about the story? Then listen and answer the questions below.

1. Who are the people in the pictures? Where are they?
2. How did Mary get into the room?
3. Why did she come to find James Bond?
4. Where did they go to talk?
5. What did Scaramanga say? What did he do?
6. Who has the golden gun?

22 Unit 3 • It all went wrong

4 Read the story. Find the lines in the text that go with each picture.

The Man with the Golden Gun

James Bond got back to his hotel room at midnight. The windows were closed and the air conditioner was on. Bond switched it off and opened the windows. His heart was still thumping in his chest. He breathed in the air with relief, then he took a shower and went to bed.

At 3:30 he was dreaming, not very peacefully, about three black-coated men with red eyes and angry white teeth. Suddenly he woke up. He listened. There was a noise. It was coming from the window. Someone was moving behind the curtain. James Bond took his gun from under his pillow, got quietly out of bed, and crept slowly along the wall toward the window. Someone was breathing behind the curtain. Bond pulled it back with one quick movement. Golden hair shone in the moonlight.

"Mary Goodnight!" Bond exclaimed. "What are *you* doing here?"

"Quick, James! Help me in!" Mary whispered urgently.

Bond put down his gun and tried to pull her through the open window. At the last moment the window banged shut with a noise like a gunshot.

"I'm really sorry, James!" Mary Goodnight whispered.

"Shh! Shh!" said Bond. He quickly led her across the room to the bathroom. First he turned on the light, then the shower. They sat down on the side of the bathtub.

"Mary," Bond asked again. "What on earth are you doing here? What's the matter?"

"James, I was so worried. An urgent message came from HQ this evening. A top KGB man, using the name Hendriks, is staying in this hotel. He knows you're here. He's looking for you!"

"I know," said Bond. "Hendriks is here all right. So is a gunman named Scaramanga. Mary, did HQ say if they have a description of me?"

"No, they don't. They just have your name, Secret Agent James Bond."

"Thanks, Mary. Now, I have to get you out of here. Don't worry about me. Just tell HQ that you gave me the message, OK?"

"OK, James." Mary Goodnight stood up and looked into his eyes. "Please be careful, James."

"Sure, sure." Bond turned off the shower and opened the bathroom door. "Now, come on!"

Suddenly a voice came from the darkness of the bedroom. "This is not your lucky day, Mr. Bond. Come here, both of you, and put your hands up!"

Scaramanga walked to the door and turned on the lights. His golden gun was pointing directly at James Bond.

5 Are these sentences true (✓) or false (✗)? Correct the false sentences.
1. James Bond felt happy to be back in his hotel room.
2. Bond was dreaming about Mary Goodnight.
3. A man with a gun woke Bond at 3:30 A.M.
4. He was very pleased to see Mary Goodnight.
5. Bond fired his gun while he was pulling Mary through the window.
6. They talked while the shower was running.
7. Bond knew that Hendriks was looking for him.
8. James helped Mary get out of the hotel.

What do you think?
- What was James Bond doing before he got back to his hotel room?
- Why did James and Mary talk in the bathroom?
- Does Mary Goodnight like James a lot?
- Does Scaramanga kill James Bond and Mary? What do you think happens next?

Language work

6 Write the past form of these verbs from the story. Which are irregular?

1. get   *got*   7. whisper _____
2. breathe _____   8. put _____
3. wake up _____   9. try _____
4. take _____   10. lead _____
5. creep _____   11. give _____
6. shine _____   12. stand up _____

7 What do these colors refer to in the story?

black   white   red   golden

Telling the story

8 Use the pictures to tell the story to a partner in your own words.

VOCABULARY

Nouns, verbs, and adjectives

1 Look at these common noun and adjective suffixes. These suffixes can be used to form different parts of speech.

Nouns	-ation -ion -ness -ity -ence -sion -ment
Adjectives	-ous -y -tific -ly -ful -less -ial

Complete the charts below and mark the stress. There are some spelling changes.

Noun	Verb
communi'cation	co'mmunicate
_____	dis'cuss
_____	'govern
invi'tation	_____
_____	de'velop
_____	ex'plain
edu'cation	_____
_____	de'cide
_____	en'joy
_____	'organize
im'provement	_____
_____	em'ploy

Noun	Adjective
'science	scien'tific
friend	_____
_____	'happy
_____	'different
'danger	_____
use	_____
help	_____
_____	'special
care	_____
noise	_____
'industry	_____
am'bition	_____

2 Complete each sentence with a word from Exercise 1.

1. My English **improved** a lot after I lived in Toronto for a month.
2. I have two _____ in life. I want to be rich, and I want to be famous.
3. "I'm going to work hard from now on." "That's a very good _____."
4. There are many _____ between my two children. They aren't similar at all.
5. Thank you for your advice. It was very _____.
6. I like Italian people. They're very nice and _____.
7. The United Nations is an international _____.
8. I asked the teacher for help, but unfortunately I didn't understand his _____.
9. Auto racing is a very _____ sport.
10. Fish soup is a _____ of this area. You must try it.
11. I'm having a party on Saturday, and I'd like to _____ you.
12. This is the _____ part of my town. There are lots of factories and businesses here.

Making negatives

3 We can make adjectives and verbs negative by using these prefixes.

Adjectives	un- im- in- il-
Verbs	un- dis-

Complete the sentences, using a word from the box and a prefix.

pack possible agree lock fair like
appear employed legal polite

1. This key doesn't work! I can't **unlock** the door.
2. I can't do math. For me, it's an _____ subject.
3. I don't _____ fish. I just prefer meat.
4. It's very _____ to ask someone how much they make.
5. When we arrived at the hotel, we _____ our suitcases.
6. I was _____ for two years. Finally, I got a job.
7. "I think learning languages is stupid." "I _____. I think it's a good idea."
8. The thief stole my bag, ran into the crowd, and _____. I never saw him again.
9. It's _____ to drive a car without a driver's license.
10. You gave her more money than me! That's _____ !

EVERYDAY ENGLISH
Time expressions

29:February 2000

1 Can you say these dates?

1/8/98   7/16/85   11/25/02

T 3.7 Listen and check.

Look at the same dates in written British English. What's the difference?

8/1/98   16/7/85   25/11/02

T 3.8 Listen and check.

2 Practice these dates. They are in American English.

June 19   August 5   July 4   March 1   February 3
1/21/88   12/2/96   4/5/80
June 11, 1965   October 18, 2000   January 31, 2005

T 3.9 Listen and check.

What days are national holidays in your country?

3 Complete these time expressions with *at*, *on*, *in*, or no preposition.

___ six o'clock	___ Saturday	___ 1995
___ last night	___ December	___ the weekend
___ Monday morning	___ the summer	___ two weeks ago
___ the evening	___ yesterday evening	___ January 18

▶▶ Grammar Reference 3.4 p. 142

4 Ask and answer the questions with a partner.

1 Do you know exactly when you were born?

> *I was born at two o'clock in the morning on Monday, June twenty-fifth, 1979.*

2 When did you last … ?
- go to the movies
- play a sport
- give someone a present
- take a vacation
- watch TV
- go to a party
- take a test
- see a lot of snow
- brush your teeth
- take a plane trip

Unit 3 • It all went wrong

4 Let's go shopping!

much/many • some/any • a few, a little, a lot of • Articles • Shopping • Prices

STARTER ▶ Play the alphabet game with things you can buy. Continue around the class.

A Yesterday I went shopping, and I bought an **a**pple.
B Yesterday I went shopping, and I bought an **a**pple and some **b**read.
C Yesterday I went shopping, and I bought an **a**pple, some **b**read, and ...

THE WEEKEND SHOPPING TRIP
Quantity

1 Sarah and Vicky are two students who share an apartment. It is Saturday morning, and Sarah has a shopping list.

T 4.1 Read and listen to the first part of their conversation.

V It says here *milk*. How much milk do we need?
S Two liters.
V And eggs? How many eggs?
S A dozen.
V And what about potatoes? How many potatoes?
S A kilo's enough.
V And butter? How much?
S Just one package.

GRAMMAR SPOT

Can we count butter?
Can we count eggs? (one egg, two eggs)
When do we say *How much ... ?*
When do we say *How many ... ?*

▶▶ Grammar Reference 4.1 p. 143

milk
eggs
potatoes
butter
bread
tomatoes
cheese
soda
frozen pizzas
jam
potato chips

2 Match these quantifiers with the items from the shopping list.

bread	200g of cheddar
tomatoes	a jar
cheese	just one loaf
soda	a bag
frozen pizzas	four or five big ones
jam	three bottles
potato chips	one pepperoni, one plain

Continue the conversation with a partner.

26 Unit 4 • Let's go shopping!

3 **T 4.2** Read and listen to the rest of Sarah and Vicky's conversation.

V Do we need anything else?
S Let's see. We have some apples, but there aren't any grapes. And there isn't any coffee, but we have some tea.
V Is there any orange juice left, or did somebody finish it?
S There's a little, but there isn't much, so we need some more.
V And vegetables? Do we have many vegetables?
S Well, I see a lot of carrots, but there aren't many onions.
V Don't forget we need a lot of potato chips and soda. My nephews are coming tomorrow!
S OK. I think that's everything. Let's go! By the way, how much money do you have? Can I borrow some?

GRAMMAR SPOT

1 Find seven count nouns (CNs) and five noncount nouns (NCs) in Exercise 3.
2 Put a check (✓) in the correct columns.

We use…	with CNs	with NCs	in affirmative sentences	in questions	in negative sentences
some	✓	✓	✓	✓ (sometimes)	✗
any					
much					
many					
lots/a lot of	✓	✓	✓	✓	✓
a few					
a little					

3 Look at the forms of *something/someone*, etc. The rules are the same as for *some* and *any* above. Find three examples in Exercise 3.

some / any	+	thing one/body where

▶▶ Grammar Reference 4.1 on p. 143

PRACTICE

Discussing grammar

1 Complete the sentences with *some* or *any*.

1. Do you have __any__ brothers or sisters?
2. We don't need _____ olive oil.
3. Here are _____ letters for you.
4. I need _____ money.
5. There aren't _____ tomatoes left.

2 Complete the sentences with *much* or *many*.

1. Do you have _____ homework?
2. We don't need _____ eggs. Just half a dozen.
3. Is there _____ traffic in your town?
4. I don't know _____ students in this class.
5. How _____ people live in your house?

3 Complete the sentences with *a little*, *a few*, or *a lot of*.

1. I have _____ close friends. Two or three.
2. He has _____ money. He's a millionaire.
3. "Do you take sugar in your coffee?" "Just _____ . Half a spoonful."
4. "Do you have _____ CDs?" "Yes, hundreds."
5. I'll be ready in _____ minutes.
6. She speaks good Spanish, but only _____ Portuguese.

Unit 4 • Let's go shopping! 27

Questions and answers

4 Look at Sarah and Vicky's bathroom. Ask and answer questions with a partner about these things:

- makeup
- shampoo
- towels
- toothbrushes
- toothpaste
- toilet paper
- hairbrushes
- soap
- bottles of perfume

Do they have much makeup? — *Lots.*

Is there any soap? — *I can't see any.*

something/someone/somewhere

5 Complete the sentences with the correct word.

some any every no	+	thing one/body where

1. "Did you meet __anyone__ nice at the party?"
   "Yes. I met _____ who knows you!"
2. "Ouch! There's _____ in my eye!"
   "Let me look. No, I can't see _____ ."
3. "Let's go _____ nice for our vacation."
   "But we can't go _____ that's too expensive."
4. "I'm so unhappy. _____ loves me."
   "I know _____ who loves you. Me."
5. I lost my glasses. I looked _____ , but I couldn't find them.
6. "Did you buy _____ when you were shopping?"
   "No, _____ . I didn't have any money."
7. I'm bored. I want _____ interesting to read, or _____ interesting to talk to, or _____ interesting to go.
8. It was a great party. _____ loved it.

T 4.3 Listen and check.

Town survey

6 Work in groups. Talk about the good things and bad things about living in your city or town. Make a list. Compare your list with the class.

> Good things
> There are a lot of cafes and restaurants.
> There are some good stores.
> We can go on lots of walks.
> Bad things
> But we don't have any good clubs.
> There aren't many ...
> There's only one ...
> There isn't anywhere that we can ...

28 Unit 4 • Let's go shopping!

THE HAPPIEST MAN I KNOW

Articles

T 4.4 Read and listen to the text.

> **GRAMMAR SPOT**
>
> 1 Find examples of the definite article (*the*) + noun and the indefinite article (*a/an*) + noun.
>
> 2 Find examples of nouns without an article. (*bread, candy*)
>
> ▶▶ Grammar Reference 4.2 p. 143

My uncle owns a general store in a small town north of Boston. The store sells a lot of things—bread, milk, fruit, vegetables, newspapers, tools, videotapes—almost everything! It is also the town post office. The children in the town always stop to buy candy or ice cream on their way home from school.

My uncle doesn't go out of town very often. He doesn't like to drive, so once a month he goes by bus to the next town and has lunch at a nice restaurant with some friends. He is one of the happiest men I know.

PRACTICE

Discussing grammar

1 In pairs, find one mistake in each sentence.
1. He's mail carrier, so he has breakfast at 4 A.M.
   He's a mail carrier, so he has breakfast at 4 a.m.
2. The love is more important than money.
3. I come to school by the bus.
4. I live in one old house in the country.
5. "Where's Jack?" "In a kitchen."
6. I live in center of town, near the hospital.
7. My parents moved to a new apartment in country.
8. I don't eat the bread because I don't like it.

2 Complete the sentences with *a/an*, *the*, or nothing.
1. I have two children, __a__ boy and _____ girl. _____ boy is 22 and _____ girl is 19.
2. Mike is _____ soldier in _____ army, and Linda is in _____ college.
3. My wife goes to _____ work by _____ train. She's _____ accountant. I don't have _____ job. I stay _____ home and take care of _____ children.
4. What _____ beautiful day! Why don't we go for _____ picnic in _____ park?
5. "What did you have for _____ lunch?" "Just _____ sandwich."

Unit 4 • Let's go shopping! 29

READING
The best shopping street in the world

1 Match a famous shopping street with a city, a store, and a product.

Street	City	Store	Product
Fifth Avenue	Hong Kong	Guerlain	sweaters
Champs-Elysées	London	Tiffany's	silk
Oxford Street	New York	Shanghai Tang	jewelry
Pedder Street	Paris	Marks and Spencer	perfume

2 Read the headline and the first paragraph of the newspaper article on page 31. Does anything surprise you? What do you want to find out when you read the article? Write some questions.

3 Read the article quickly and answer the questions you wrote in Exercise 2 above.

What is the best summary of the article?

Nowy Swiat is the best shopping street in the world because …
- ☐ … so many Polish people go walking there.
- ☐ … it is a pleasant place to go shopping, and the stores are small.
- ☐ … everything is very expensive and very exclusive.
- ☐ … the stores sell quality goods that you can't buy anywhere else.

4 Read the article again and answer the questions.
1. How do we know that Nowy Swiat is the most popular shopping street?
2. Why is it such a nice place to go shopping?
3. What can you see in the photos that is described in the article?
4. Why don't a lot of foreign people go to Nowy Swiat?
5. Why are the things produced by Polish manufacturers so good?
6. What can you buy here? What can't you buy?
7. What is expensive? What isn't expensive?
8. What's good about *Cafe Blikle*?
9. What is special about the stores on Nowy Swiat?

Language work

Complete the sentences with two different ideas from the article.

On Nowy Swiat, there are a lot of …   *There isn't any …*
There aren't any/many …   *There are some …*

What do you think?

- What are some of the famous brands and products that you can buy in many countries of the world? Think of clothes, food, cars, etc. Make a list. Work in groups and choose the most famous three. Compare your list with the class.
- What is the main shopping street in your city or town? What can you buy there that's special?
- Do you enjoy shopping? What do you like shopping for? What *don't* you like shopping for?

30 Unit 4 • Let's go shopping!

The best shopping street in the world

No, it isn't Oxford Street, the Champs-Elysées, or even Fifth Avenue. A new survey shows that the most popular shopping street in the world is ... Nowy Swiat. Where's that? In Warsaw, Poland, of course.

by ANNE APPLEBAUM

"If you're tired, stop at Cafe Blikle."

"There are a lot of small, chic shops."

A recent survey has shown that the busiest shopping street in the world is not in London, New York, or Paris, but in Warsaw. It's called Nowy Swiat (pronounced /ˈnavi ʃviət/) which means *New World*. An incredible 14,000 Poles walk down this main street every hour.

It is a wonderful place to shop. The sidewalks are very wide. There are statues, palaces, attractive townhouses, exclusive cafes, and stylish restaurants. The buildings aren't too tall. They look old, but in fact the whole city was rebuilt after World War II.

There aren't any billboards or neon lights. There isn't any loud music, and there aren't many tourists. People think that Polish stores have nothing to sell, so nobody goes shopping here. The world doesn't know about this paradise for shoppers—yet.

It is now possible to buy almost everything in Warsaw. There are a lot of stores from the West, but the interesting thing is that Polish manufacturers are now producing high quality goods. They are good because they are not mass produced for world consumption.

Nowy Swiat has a lot of small stores, specialty stores, chic stores. It doesn't have the huge department stores that sell the same things everywhere.

If you want an exquisite handmade suit, Nowy Swiat is the place to go. It isn't cheap. You will pay up to $2,000. For beautiful French baby clothes, go to *Petit Bateau*. You will pay $75 for a pair of baby blue jeans. A dress for a baby girl is about $150. At *Désa*, a famous antique store, a desk costs $8,000, and a nineteenth century Russian icon is $300.

Not everything is expensive. At a store called *Pantera* you can buy leather goods—handbags, purses, coats, and belts. *Cepelia* specializes in folk art. There are also bookstores and record stores. And there are a lot of small boutiques that sell men's and women's clothes that aren't too expensive.

If you're tired, stop at *Cafe Blikle*. This is a fashionable place to meet. You'll find a lively atmosphere and a lot of well-known Poles. The frozen yogurt and ice cream are both excellent, and its famous doughnuts are delicious.

It is possible to travel the world and find the same things for sale in every country. But Warsaw is different because its stores are unique—and they're on Nowy Swiat.

VOCABULARY AND LISTENING
Buying things

1 What can you buy or do in these places? Write two more things for each place.
Compare your ideas with the class.

a cafe	a clothing store	a bank	a newsstand	a drugstore
drink coffee	buy jeans	exchange money	buy a magazine	buy makeup

2 **T 4.5** You will hear four conversations. Listen to each conversation and answer the questions.
1. Where is the conversation taking place? Choose from one of the places in Exercise 1.
2. What does the customer want?
3. Can the sales clerk/cashier help?
4. How much does the customer pay?

3 Complete these lines from the conversations. Look at the tapescript on page 130 and check your answers.

1. **A** Hello. Can I help you?
   B I _____ , thanks.
   …
   B I'm looking for a sweater _____ . Do you have _____ ?
   A I'll take a look. _____ are you?
   B Medium.
   A Here you are.
   B That's great. _____ ?
   A Of course. The fitting rooms are over there.
   …
   B I like it.
   A It _____ .
   B How much is it?
   A $59.99.
   B OK. I _____ .
   A How would you like to pay?
   B _____ .

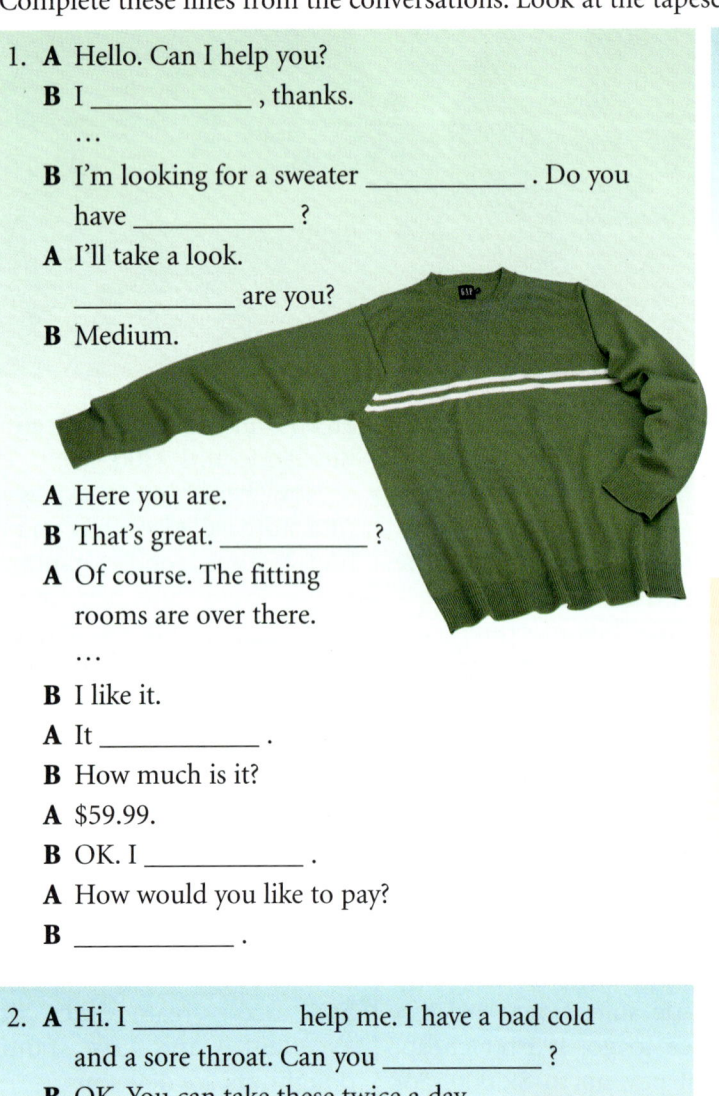

2. **A** Hi. I _____ help me. I have a bad cold and a sore throat. Can you _____ ?
   B OK. You can take these twice a day.
   A Thank you. _____ some tissues _____ ?
   B Sure. _____ ?
   A No, that's all, thanks.
   B OK. That's _____ .

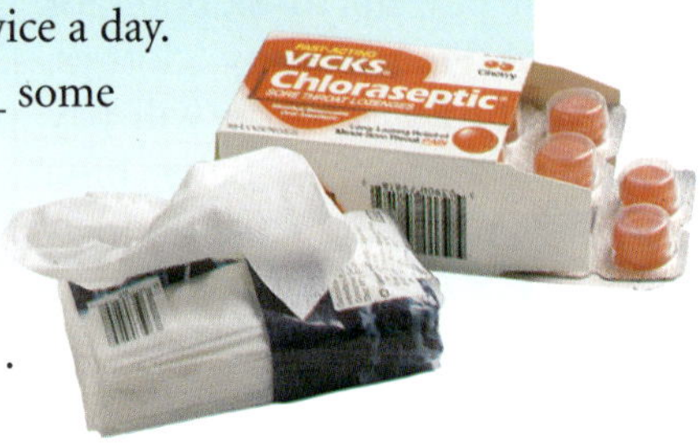

3. **A** _____ help me? I'm looking for this month's issue of *Vogue*. Can you tell me _____ ?
   B Right there on the middle rack. Next to *Latina*.
   A Thanks.
   B That's $3.50.

4. **A** Good morning. Can I have a _____ , please?
   B With sugar?
   A No, thanks. Oh, and a doughnut, please.
   B _____ there aren't _____ . We have some delicious muffins.
   A I'll have a blueberry muffin.
   B Will _____ today?
   A That's it.
   B _____ , please.
   A OK.

32 Unit 4 • Let's go shopping!

EVERYDAY ENGLISH
Prices and shopping

1 Practice the way we write and say prices in US currency.

American English		British English	
Written	Spoken	Written	Spoken
$1.00	a dollar	£1	a pound
50¢	fifty cents	50p	fifty p
$1.99	a dollar ninety-nine	£1.99	one pound ninety-nine
$16.40	sixteen-forty/sixteen dollars and forty cents	£16.40	sixteen pounds forty

T 4.6 Listen to the conversations and write the prices you hear.

1. $6.00   2. _____   3. _____   4. _____   5. _____   6. _____

2 What's the current exchange rate between US dollars and your currency?

There are about five … to the dollar.

In your country, how much is … ?

- a pair of jeans
- a CD
- a hamburger
- a liter of gas

3 Make conversations in these places with a partner. You can use the ideas to help you.

1. in a clothing store
a shirt/tie
What size are you?
Small/medium/large
too small/too big/just right
No, thanks./I'll take it.

2. in a post office
some stamps
First class or express mail?
a letter/postcard to …
send this package to …
by air/by surface mail

3. in a cafe
a black/light coffee
an espresso/a cappuccino
a pot of tea
a fruit juice
a bottle of mineral water
a piece of chocolate cake

4. in a drugstore
I have a stomachache/ sore throat
conditioner
shaving cream
deodorant

Unit 4 • Let's go shopping! 33

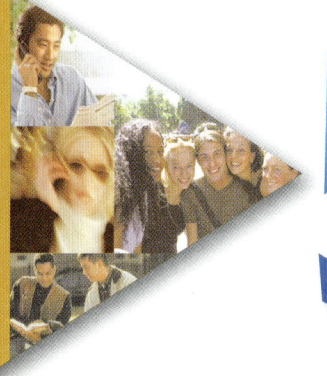

5 What do you want to do?

Verb patterns 1 • Future forms • Hot verbs • How do you feel?

STARTER Complete these sentences with ideas about you.
- Someday I want to ...
- Right now, I'd like to ...
- I enjoy ... because I like ...
- I can ... but I can't ...
- Tonight I'm going to ...

HOPES AND AMBITIONS
Verb patterns 1

1 Take a guess. Who do you think said each line below? Match the people with their hopes and ambitions.

1. ___ "I'd like to have my own business, something like a flying school."
2. ___ "I'm going to be an astronaut and fly to Mars."
3. ___ "I'm looking forward to having more time to do the things I want to do."
4. ___ "I would love to have one of my plays performed on Broadway."
5. ___ "We hope to find work as we go around the world."
6. ___ "We're thinking of moving, because the kids will be leaving home soon."

T 5.1 Listen and check.

2 Complete the chart.

	Ambitions/Plans	Reasons
Duane		
Maria		
Jim		
Martin		
Amy		
Helen		

3 Underline the examples of verb + verb in Exercise 1.
  <u>I'd like to have</u> my own business.

Look at the tapescript on page 130. Find more examples of verb + verb.

a Duane, 9
c Jim, 29
d Martin, 39
e Amy, 49

GRAMMAR SPOT

1 Complete the sentences with the words *go abroad*. Put the verb *go* in the correct form.

  I want **to go abroad.**
  I'd like ...
  I can't ...
  I'm looking forward to ...
  I hope ...
  I enjoy ...
  I'm thinking of ...
  I'd love ...

2 What's the difference between these sentences?

  I like going to the movies.
  I'd like to go to the movies tonight.

▶▶ Grammar Reference 5.1 and 5.2 p. 144

PRACTICE

Discussing grammar

1 In these sentences, one or two verbs are correct, but not all three. Put a check (✓) next to the correct verbs.

1. I _____ to write poetry.
   a. ✓ want   b. ☐ enjoy   c. ✓ 'd like
2. We _____ going to Hawaii for our vacation.
   a. ☐ are hoping   b. ☐ 're thinking of   c. ☐ like
3. I _____ go home early tonight.
   a. ☐ want   b. ☐ like   c. ☐ can
4. I _____ to see you again soon.
   a. ☐ hope   b. ☐ 'd like   c. ☐ 'm looking forward
5. Do you _____ learning English?
   a. ☐ want   b. ☐ enjoy   c. ☐ like
6. We _____ taking a few days off soon.
   a. ☐ 're thinking of   b. ☐ 'd love to   c. ☐ 're looking forward to

Make correct sentences with the other verbs.

I enjoy writing poetry.

Making questions

2 Complete the questions.

1. **A** I hope to go to college.
   B (What/want/study?) **What do you want to study?**
2. **A** One of my favorite hobbies is cooking.
   B (What/like/make?) _____
3. **A** I get terrible headaches.
   B (When/start/get/them?) _____
4. **A** We're planning our vacation now.
   B (Where/think of/go?) _____
5. **A** I'm tired.
   B (What/like/do/tonight?) _____

T 5.2 Listen and check. What are **A**'s answers? Practice the conversations with a partner.

Talking about you

3 Ask and answer the questions with a partner.

- What do you like doing on vacation?
- Where would you like to be right now?
- Do you like learning English?
- Would you like to take a break now?

4 Ask and answer questions about your future plans and ambitions.

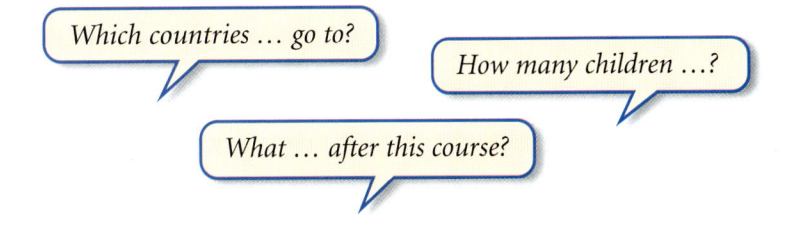

Which countries ... go to?

How many children ...?

What ... after this course?

Unit 5 • What do you want to do? 35

FUTURE INTENTIONS
going to and *will*

1 Match the pictures and sentences.

1. ☐ They're going to watch a baseball game.
2. ☐ I'll pick it up for you.
3. ☐ She's going to travel around the world.
4. ☐ Oh! I'll answer it.
5. ☐ Don't worry. I'll lend you some.
6. ☐ We're going out for dinner.

2 Add a line before and after the sentences in Exercise 1.

Before

I don't have any money.
What's Sue doing next year?
The phone's ringing.
Darn it! I dropped one.
What are you and Pete doing tonight?
What are the guys doing this afternoon?

After

Thank you. That's very nice of you.
I'm expecting a call.
Thanks. I'll pay you back tomorrow. I won't forget.
Lucky her!
The Chicago Cubs are playing.
It's my birthday.

T 5.3 Listen and check. Practice the conversations with a partner.

GRAMMAR SPOT

1 Notice the forms of *will*.
   I'**ll** = short form
   I **won't** = negative

2 All the sentences in Exercise 1 express intentions.
   • Three intentions are spontaneous
     (= made at the moment of speaking).
     Which are they?
   • Three intentions are premeditated
     (= made before the moment of speaking).
     What happened **before** each one?

   ▶▶ Grammar Reference 5.3 p. 144

36 Unit 5 • What do you want to do?

PRACTICE

Let's have a party!

1 Your class has decided to have a party. Everyone has to help. Say at least five things you'll do.

I'll bring the music.

I'll buy some potato chips.

2 Your teacher didn't hear what you said. Listen to your teacher and correct him/her.

Teacher

I'll bring some music.

Oh, all right. Well, I'll buy some potato chips.

You

*No, **I'm** going to bring some music!*

*No, **I'm** going to buy some potato chips!*

Discussing grammar

3 Choose the correct verb form.
   1. "My bag is so heavy."
      "Give it to me. *I'll carry* / *I'm going to carry* it for you."
   2. I bought some warm boots because *I'll go* / *I'm going* skiing.
   3. "Tony's back from vacation."
      "He is? *I'll give* / *I'm going to give* him a call."
   4. "What are you doing tonight?"
      "*We'll see* / *We're going to see* a play at the theater."
   5. "Are you coming to our class party?"
      "Yes, *I'll see* / *I'm going to see* you there."
   6. Congratulations! I hear *you'll get married* / *you're going to get married*.
   7. "I need to mail these letters."
      I'll mail / *I'm going to mail* them for you."
   8. "Where are you going on your vacation this year?"
      "*We will go to* / *We're going to* Hawaii."

4 **T 5.4** Close your books. Listen to the beginnings of the conversations from Exercise 3 and complete them.

Check it

5 Correct the sentences.
   1. What you want drink?
   2. I have a soda, please.
   3. I can't to help you.
   4. It's starting rain.
   5. I'm looking forward to see you again soon.
   6. I think to change my job soon.
   7. Call me tonight. I give you my phone number.
   8. I go have a big party for my next birthday.

Talking about you

6 Talk to a partner about your plans for tonight, tomorrow, next weekend, your next vacation, New Year's …

What are you doing tonight / going to do tonight?

Where are you going … ?

I'm going to stay home and …

I'm going to see …

I think I'll …

Unit 5 • What do you want to do? 37

READING
Hollywood kids

1 What are some of the problems of being a teenager? Put a check (✓) in the boxes on the left.

- ☐ drugs ☐
- ☐ violence in the streets ☐
- ☐ they don't have enough money ☐
- ☐ their parents don't give them enough attention ☐
- ☐ they worry about how they look ☐
- ☐ they have no interests or ambitions ☐
- ☐ their parents want them to do well in life ☐
- ☐ they're too old to be children, but too young to be adults ☐

2 Read the text about Hollywood kids. What are some of their problems? Put a check (✓) in the boxes on the right. Are there any differences?

3 Are these sentences true (✓) or false (✗)? Correct the false sentences.
   1. Everyone in Hollywood is rich and famous.
   2. Hollywood kids don't lead ordinary lives.
   3. They understand the value of what they have.
   4. Trent Maguire is ambitious.
   5. The adults try hard to be good parents.
   6. Amanda's mother listens to all her daughter's problems.
   7. The kids are often home alone.
   8. Their parents organize every part of their lives.
   9. The kids don't want to be children.
   10. All the kids complain about living in Hollywood.

4 Answer the questions.
   1. In what way do Rachel, Lindsey, and Trent live unreal lives?
   2. Does anything surprise you about what the kids say?
   3. What are their ambitions?

What do you think?

- Do you feel sorry for children in Hollywood? Is there anything about their lives that you would like?
- What is your opinion of their parents?
- Do teenagers around the world think the same as Hollywood kids?
- Do you think it is dangerous to have everything you want?

Hollywood
What's it like

In Hollywood, the home of the entertainment industry, it seems like everybody wants to be rich, famous, and beautiful. Nobody wants to be old, unknown, or poor. For kids growing up in such a world, life can be difficult. Their parents are ambitious, and the children are part of the parents' ambitions.

Parents pay for extravagant parties, expensive cars, and designer clothes. The children have everything, but never learn the value of anything because it all comes so easy. A 13-year-old boy, Trent Maguire, has a driver, credit cards, and unlimited cash to do what he wants when he wants. "Someday, I'll make more than my Dad," he boasts.

Parents buy care and attention for their children because they have no time to give it themselves. Amanda's mother employs a bodyguard/chauffeur, a personal trainer, a nutritionist, a singing coach, and a counselor to take care of all of her 15-year-old daughter's needs.

Often there is no parent at home most days, so children decide whether to make their own meals or go out to restaurants, when to watch television or do homework. They organize their own social lives. There's no place for childhood games. Children become adults before they're ready.

Hollywood has always been a place where dreams come true. Lots of Hollywood kids live in a world where money, beauty, and pleasure are the only gods. Will children around the world soon start to think the same? Or do they already?

Looks are very important in Hollywood. If you're good-looking, you'll go far. I want to be a beautician. You grow up really fast here. Everyone is in a rush to be an adult, to be going to clubs. It's not cool to be a kid. **Melissa, age 18** ▼

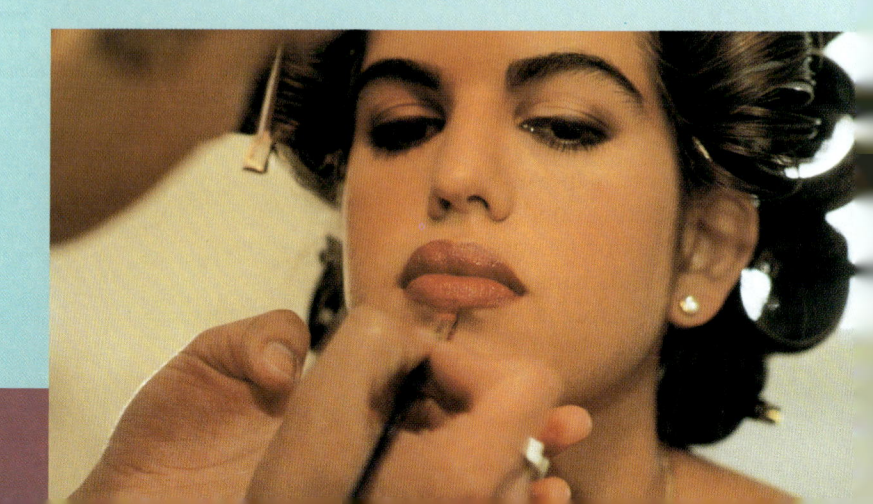

kids
when you have it all?

By Lonnie Feldman

"I live in a hotel and when I come home from school, there are maybe 80 people who say 'Good day' to me. It's their job to say that. In the bathroom there are mirrors everywhere. I love looking at myself. I can spend five hours doing my hair and posing. I'm going to be a model."
Rachel, age 10 ▶

▲ "I've wanted to get my nose done since I was 12. My friends started having plastic surgery and liposuction during my freshman year of high school. My nose cost $10,000. But it was worth it. It changed my life. I'm gonna get into the movies."
Lindsey, age 18

VOCABULARY
Hot verbs—have, go, come

1. The verbs *have*, *go*, and *come* are very common in English. Look at these examples from the text on pages 38–39.

have	go	come
... they have no time ... The children have everything ...	You'll go far. ... going to clubs.	... it all comes so easy. ... a place where dreams come true.

2. Put *have*, *go*, or *come* into each blank.

   __have__ an accident   _____ a cold
   _____ in first in a race   _____ wrong
   _____ out for a meal   _____ a meeting
   _____ and see me   _____ abroad
   _____ shopping

3. Fill in the blanks with the correct form of *have*, *go*, or *come*.

   1. We're __having__ a party next Saturday. Would you like _____ ?
   2. I _____ a terrible headache. Can I _____ home, please?
   3. You must see my new apartment. _____ over and _____ a drink sometime.
   4. "I'm _____ out now, Mom. Bye!" "OK. _____ a good time. What time are you _____ home?"
   5. Hi, Dave. Pete _____ breakfast right now. I'll _____ and tell him you're here.
   6. _____ on! Get out of bed. It's time _____ to school.
   7. It's a beautiful day. Let's _____ to the park. We can _____ a picnic.
   8. I'm _____ skiing next week. Do you _____ any ski clothes I could borrow?

LISTENING
You've got a friend

1. Who says these things? Write *1*, *2*, or *3*.
   1. Your best friend
   2. Your boyfriend/girlfriend
   3. Your ex-boyfriend/ex-girlfriend

   ____ I'll love you forever.
   ____ I'll never forget you.
   ____ I'll always be there for you.
   ____ I'll always remember the times we had together.
   ____ I'll do anything for you.
   ____ You'll never find anyone who loves you more than I do.

2. Listen to the first verse of the song. Discuss these questions.
   1. Do you think the man and woman live together?
   2. Is it a close relationship?
   3. What is the relationship between them now? What do you think it was in the past?

3. **T 5.5** Listen and complete the song.

You've Got a Friend, by Carole King

When you're down and troubled
And you need a _____
And nothing, but _____
Close your eyes and think of me
And soon I _____
To brighten up even your darkest nights.
(Chorus)
You just call out my name,
and you know wherever I am
I _____ to see you again.
Winter, spring, _____
All you have to do is call
And I'll be there, yeah, yeah, yeah,
You've got a friend.
If the sky above you
_____ and full of clouds
And that old north _____
Keep your head together
And _____
And soon I'll be knocking on your door.
Hey, _____ that you've got a friend?
People can be so cold.
_____ and desert you.
Well they'll take your soul if you let them.
Oh, yeah, but _____ .
(Chorus)

EVERYDAY ENGLISH
How do you feel?

1 Look at the photos. How do the people feel?

2 All the lines in **A** answer the question *How are you?* Match a line in **A** with a line in **B**.

A	B
1. I feel nervous.	It's so wet and miserable.
2. I don't feel very well.	I'm going on vacation to Bangkok tomorrow.
3. I'm feeling a lot better, thanks.	My grandfather's going into the hospital for tests.
4. I'm really excited.	I think I'm getting the flu.
5. I'm sick of this weather.	Nothing's going right in my life.
6. I'm really tired.	I have a test today.
7. I'm kind of worried.	I have a lot more energy.
8. I feel really depressed right now.	I didn't sleep very well last night.

3 Choose a reply for each set of sentences in Exercise 2.
   ___ a. Cheer up! Things can't be that bad!
   ___ b. Why don't you go home and go to bed?
   ___ c. I'm sorry to hear that, but I'm sure he'll be all right.
   ___ d. I know. We really need some sun.
   ___ e. That happens to me sometimes. I just read in bed.
   _1_ f. Good luck! Do your best.
   ___ g. That's good. I'm glad to hear it.
   ___ h. That's great. Have a good time.

T 5.6 Listen and compare your answers.

4 Make more conversations with a partner about these things:
- a wedding
- a visit to the dentist
- problems with parents or teenage children
- a letter from the bank
- a big project at work or school
- an argument with a boyfriend/girlfriend

Unit 5 · What do you want to do? 41

6 The best in the world

What ... like? • *Comparatives and superlatives* • *Synonyms and antonyms* • *Directions*

STARTER

1 What is the capital city of your country? What is the population? Is it an old or modern city?

2 Write down two things that you like about your capital and two things that you don't like.

> *I like traveling on the subway in Washington, D.C., but I don't like the buses. They're too slow.*

WORLD TRAVEL
What's it like?

1 Read about Todd Bridges.

2 What do you know about the three cities in the chart below? Where are they?

3 **T 6.1** Listen to what Todd says about Melbourne, Dubai, and Paris. Write the adjectives he uses for each city. Compare with a partner.

Melbourne	Dubai	Paris
big		
beautiful		

GRAMMAR SPOT

1 Match the questions and answers.

	It's beautiful.
Do you like Paris?	Yes, I do.
What's Paris like?	It has lots of old buildings.
	No, I don't.

2 Which question in 1 means: *Tell me about Paris*.

▶▶ Grammar Reference 6.1 p. 145

4 Work with a partner. Ask and answer questions about the places Todd visited.

> *What's Melbourne like?*

> *It's ...*   *It has ...*   *There are ...*

TODD BRIDGES

Todd Bridges is only 17 years old, but he is already a successful tennis player. He comes from Chicago, but he travels all over the world playing tennis. Last year he played in tennis championships in **Melbourne**, **Dubai**, and **Paris**.

42 Unit 6 • The best in the world

PRACTICE

What's Chicago like?

1 You are asking Todd about Chicago. Complete the questions with *is* or *are* and the correct words from the box.

| the restaurants   the people   the weather |
| the nightlife   the buildings |

1. **You** What **'s the weather** like?
   Todd Well, Chicago's called "the windy city," and it really can be windy!
2. **You** What _____ like?
   Todd They're very interesting. You meet people from all over the world.
3. **You** What _____ like?
   Todd A lot of them are very, very tall. The Sears Tower is 110 stories high.
4. **You** What _____ like?
   Todd They're very good. You can find food from every country in the world.
5. **You** What _____ like?
   Todd Oh, it's wonderful. There's lots to do in Chicago.

2 **T 6.2** Listen and check. Practice with a partner.

3 Ask and answer the same questions about the town or city you are in now.

BIG, BIGGER, BIGGEST!
Comparatives and superlatives

1 Read the second part of the conversation with Todd. He compares the places he visited last year. Can you complete any of the sentences?

"Melbourne was interesting, but for me, Paris was _____ interesting _____ Melbourne, and in some ways Dubai was the _____ interesting of all because it was so different _____ any other place I know. It was also the _____, driest, and _____ modern. It was hot in Melbourne but not _____ hot _____ in Dubai. Dubai was _____ hotter! Melbourne is _____ older _____ Dubai but not _____ old _____ Paris. Paris was _____ oldest city I visited, but it has some great modern buildings, too. It was the _____ romantic place. I loved it."

T 6.3 Listen and check.

Unit 6 · The best in the world   43

GRAMMAR SPOT

1 What are the comparative and superlative forms of the following adjectives? What are the rules?

   a. small   c. busy
       cold   noisy
       near   dry

   b. big   d. beautiful
       hot   interesting
       wet   exciting

2 These adjectives are irregular. What are the comparative and superlative forms?

> far   good   bad

3 Adjectives also combine with *as ... as*.
   Dubai isn't **as** cosmopolitan **as** Chicago.

▶▶ **Grammar Reference 6.2 p. 145**

---

2 **T 6.4** Listen and repeat the sentences.

/hɑtər ðən/
This summer's hotter than last.

/əz hɑt əz/
It wasn't as hot as this last year.

3 Practice these sentences with a partner.

> It isn't as warm today as it was yesterday.
> But it's warmer than it was last week.
> I'm not as tall as you, but I'm taller than Ana.
> My car's more expensive than John's.
> But it isn't as expensive as Ana's.

T 6.5 Listen and check.

4 Learn this poem by heart.

> Good, better, best.
> Never, never rest
> 'til your good is better,
> And your better best.

PRACTICE

Comparing four capital cities

1 Match the cities and the photographs. Of which countries are these the capital cities?

> Washington, D.C.   Tokyo   Stockholm   Brasilia

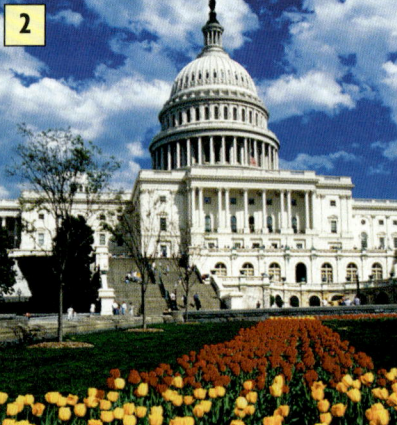

2 Work with a partner.

Student A Go to page 119 and read about Tokyo and Washington, D.C.
Student B Go to page 121 and read about Stockholm and Brasilia.

Conversations

3 Work with a partner and continue these conversations.

1. **A** I moved to a new apartment last week.
   B Really? What's it like?
   A Well, it's _bigger_ than my old one but it isn't as modern and …

2. **A** I hear Sandy and Al broke up.
   B Yeah. Sandy has a new boyfriend.
   A Really? What's he like?
   B Well, he's _____ than Al and …

3. **A** We have a new teacher.
   B Really? What's she like?
   A Well, I think she's the _____ teacher we've ever had …

4. **A** Did you get a new car?
   B Well, it's secondhand, but it's new to me.
   A What's it like?
   B Well, it's _____ than my old car …

Act out a conversation for the class. Whose conversation is the longest?

T 6.6 Listen and compare. Repeat the last lines.

Check it

4 Correct the sentences.
1. He's more older than he looks.
2. Laura's as tall than her mother.
3. "What does Las Vegas like?" "It's really exciting!"
4. Trains in Tokyo are more crowded that in Washington, D.C.
5. Harvard is one of oldest universities in North America.
6. This is more hard than I expected.
7. Who is the most rich person in the world?
8. Everything is more cheap in my country.

LISTENING AND SPEAKING
Living in another country

1 What do you know about Sweden? What is the country like? What are the people like? Discuss these statements about Sweden. Do you think they are true (✓) or false (✗)?

1. In winter there is only one hour of daylight.
2. Swedish people look forward to winter.
3. The houses are cold in winter.
4. In Sweden, it gets much hotter in summer than in New York or Washington, D.C.
5. In parts of Sweden the sun never sets from May to July.
6. Many people in the United States work longer hours than people in Sweden.
7. Swedes always start work early in the morning.
8. Country cottages in Sweden are usually very luxurious.
9. All houses have a sauna.
10. The whole family likes to sit in the sauna together.

2 **T 6.7** You are going to listen to Jane talking to her friend about her life in Sweden. Jane comes from the United States, but three years ago she married a Swede and went to live and work in Stockholm. Listen and check your answers to Exercise 1.

3 Compare your country with what you learn about Sweden.

In my country it gets dark at five o'clock in winter, and it's much warmer than in Sweden.

Unit 6 • The best in the world 45

READING AND SPEAKING
A tale of two millionaires

1. Who are the richest people in your country? Where does their money come from? How do they spend their money?

2. Match the verbs and nouns. Many of them have to do with money.

Verbs	Nouns
1. make	a bank account
2. spoil	poverty
3. wear	a thief
4. open	a will
5. live in	stocks and bonds
6. inherit	a child
7. buy	a leg
8. arrest	ragged clothes
9. invest	a lot of money from someone
10. amputate	a lot of money in something

3. You are going to read about two millionaires. One was very stingy, the other very generous. First read *quickly* about Milton Petrie. Can you remember any examples of his kindness?

4. Now read *quickly* about Hetty Green. Can you remember any examples of her stinginess?

5. Work with a partner.

   Student A Read about Milton Petrie.
   Student B Read about Hetty Green.

   Answer the questions with your partner.
   1. When were Milton and Hetty born?
   2. What were their parents like?
   3. How did Milton and Hetty become so wealthy?
   4. Who wore ragged clothes?
   5. What was the stingiest thing Hetty did?
   6. Why did Milton like making a lot of money?
   7. Who did they marry?
   8. When did they die? How old were they?
   9. Who left the most money? Who did they leave it to?

What do you think?

Discuss these questions in small groups.
- How were Milton and Hetty's childhoods different?
- How did their childhoods affect them later?
- Why was Milton especially generous to police officers?
- Why did Hetty's daughter build a hospital?
- What was the kindest thing Milton did?
- Who had the happier life? Milton or Hetty?

A tale of
Some millionaires

Milton Petrie

The Most Generous Man in the World

Every morning, billionaire Milton Petrie walked from his New York apartment and bought a newspaper from the ragged old man on the street corner. One morning the man wasn't there. Petrie learned that he was very ill in the city hospital. Immediately he paid his hospital bill and later, when the man died, paid for his funeral.

Milton with the model he helped

two millionaires

spend it and some save it. **Elizabeth Wilson** reports on one of each.

The old man was just one of many people that Milton Petrie helped with his money. Whenever he read about personal disasters in the newspaper, Petrie sent generous checks, especially to the families of police officers or fire fighters injured at work. He also sent checks to a mother who lost five children in a fire, and a beautiful model, whose face was cut in a knife attack. It cost him millions of dollars, but he still had millions left. He said that he was lucky in business and he wanted to help those less fortunate than himself. "The nice thing is, the harder I work, the more money I make, and the more people I can help."

Milton Petrie died in 1994, when he was 92. His will was 120 pages long because he left $150 million to 383 people. His widow, Carroll, his fourth and last wife, said his generosity was a result of the poverty of his early years. His family was poor but kindhearted. His father was a Russian immigrant who became a police officer, but he never arrested anyone; he was too kind. He couldn't even give out a parking ticket.

Hetty Green

The Richest, Stingiest Woman in the World

Henrietta (Hetty) Green was a very spoiled, only child. She was born in Massachusetts in 1835. Her father was a millionaire businessman. Her mother was often ill, and so from the age of two her father took her with him to work and taught her about stocks and bonds. At the age of six she started reading the daily financial newspapers and she opened her own bank account.

Her father died when she was 21, and she inherited $7.5 million. She went to New York and invested on Wall Street. Hetty saved every penny, eating in the cheapest restaurants for 15 cents. She became one of the richest and most hated women in the world. She was called "The Witch of Wall Street." At 33 she married Edward Green, a multi-millionaire, and had two children, Ned and Sylvia.

Hetty's stinginess was legendary. She always argued about prices in stores. She walked to the local grocery store to buy broken cookies that were much cheaper, and to get a free bone for her much loved dog, Dewey. Once she lost a two-cent stamp and spent the whole night looking for it. She never bought clothes and always wore the same long, ragged black skirt. Worst of all, when her son, Ned, fell and injured his knee, she refused to pay for a doctor and spent hours looking for free medical help. In the end Ned's leg was amputated.

When she died in 1916 she left her children $100 million (worth $9.3 billion today). Her daughter built a hospital with her money.

VOCABULARY AND PRONUNCIATION

Synonyms

1 We often use synonyms in conversation because we don't want to repeat words.

*It's a **beautiful** day today!*

*Yes, it's really **nice** out.*

Complete the conversations using an adjective of similar meaning from the box.

sick of   generous   great   enormous   modern   wealthy

1. **A** "Mary's family is very rich."
   B "Well, I knew her uncle was very _wealthy_."
2. **A** "Look at all these new buildings!"
   B "Yes. This city's much more _____ than I expected."
3. **A** "Wasn't that movie wonderful?"
   B "Yes, it was _____."
4. **A** "George doesn't have much money, but he's so thoughtful."
   B "Yes, he is. He's one of the most _____ people I know."
5. **A** "Steve and Elaine's house is huge."
   B "Yes, it's absolutely _____."
6. **A** "I'm bored with this lesson!"
   B "I know, I'm really _____ it, too!"

2 **T 6.8** Listen and check. Listen again, paying particular attention to the stress and intonation. Practice the conversations with a partner.

Antonyms

3 We can also use antonyms in conversation to avoid repeating words.

*What an **awful** meal!*

*I know. It wasn't very **good**, was it?*

Match the following adjectives with their *two* opposites in Exercise 1.

interested	bored	sick of
awful	_____	_____
stingy	_____	_____
old	_____	_____
poor	_____	_____
tiny	_____	_____

4 Sometimes it is more polite to use *not very* and an opposite adjective.

Tom is short.   *Tom **isn't very** tall.*
His clothes are dirty. *His clothes **aren't very** clean.*

Restate these sentences using *not very*.

1. Mark's apartment is tiny.
2. Paul and Sue are stingy.
3. This TV show is boring.
4. Their children are rude.
5. John looks miserable.
6. His sister is stupid.

5 **T 6.9** Listen and check. Pay particular attention to the stress and intonation. Practice with your partner.

EVERYDAY ENGLISH
Directions

1 Look at the map of Pleasantville and find these things:
- a park
- woods
- a pond
- a path
- a hill
- a bridge
- a gate

2 Read these descriptions and add the places to the map.

| coffee shop (x2) | hotel | bank |
| supermarket | flower shop | |

1. The hotel is on Station Road, across from the train station.
2. The bank is on the corner of Main Street and Hill Road. It is next to the pharmacy.
3. The supermarket is between the bakery and the furniture store.
4. There is a bus stop in front of the flower shop.
5. There are two coffee shops. The Big Jolt is on Eastern Avenue, behind the movie theater, and the Java is on Station Road, across from the flower shop.

3 Ask and answer questions with a partner about the other places. Use the prepositions from Exercise 2.

> Where's the library?

> It's on the corner of Station Road and Eastern Avenue, across from the flower shop.

4 Complete the directions from the tennis court to the museum with the prepositions in the box. Look at the map to help you.

| past   up   down   over   into (x2)   out of   across   through (x2) |

You go __down__ the path, _____ the pond, _____ the bridge, and _____ the gate. Then you go _____ the road. Take the path _____ the park and _____ the woods. When you come _____ the woods, just follow the path _____ the steps and _____ the museum. It takes about five minutes or less.

T 6.10 Listen and check.

5 Give your partner directions to get to your home from your school.

7 Fame

Present Perfect • *for, since* • Adverbs, word pairs • Short answers

STARTER What is the Past Simple and the past participle of these verbs?

sing   be   sell   win   have   hear   do   eat   know   break

FAMOUS SINGERS
Present Perfect and Past Simple

1 Look at the photographs of two well-known American singers. How do you think they are related?

Complete the sentences with *He* or *She*.

1. **He** sang pop music and jazz. **She** sings jazz, pop, and rhythm & blues.
2. _____ recorded more than 600 songs and sold over 50 million records. _____ has made over 17 albums so far.
3. _____ was born in Los Angeles and has lived in California for most of her life. _____ was born in Montgomery, Alabama, grew up in Chicago, then later moved to California.
4. _____ has been married twice and has one son. _____ married for the first time in 1976. _____ was married twice and had five children.

T 7.1 Listen and check.

GRAMMAR SPOT

1 Find examples of the Past Simple in the four sentences above.
Find examples of the Present Perfect.

2 Complete the rule.
We make the Present Perfect with the auxiliary verb _____ + the _____ .

3 Why are different tenses used in these sentences?
Nat King Cole **recorded** more than 600 songs.
Natalie Cole **has recorded** 17 albums.

▶▶ Grammar Reference 7.1 and 7.2 p. 146

Nat King Cole (1919–1965)

50 Unit 7 • Fame

2 Put the verbs in the Present Perfect or Past Simple.
1. Nat King Cole __won__ (win) many awards, including a Grammy Award in 1959 and Capitol Records' "Tower of Achievement" award. Natalie Cole _____ (win) eight Grammies and many other awards for her singing.
2. He _____ (have) his own TV show in 1956 and _____ (appear) in a number of movies. She _____ (appear) in several TV specials and TV movies.
3. She _____ (receive) a degree in psychology from the University of Massachusetts in 1972. She _____ (live) mostly in California since then.
4. She _____ (be) a recording artist for more than 25 years. She _____ (record) her first album, *Inseparable*, in 1975. With that album she _____ (win) two Grammy Awards in 1976.
5. Her remarkable album, *Unforgettable with Love*, _____ (come) out in 1991. On it, she sings a "duet" with her father's voice of the song "Unforgettable." Since then, the album _____ (sell) over five million copies.

T 7.2 Listen and check.

Natalie Cole (1950–)

3 Here are the answers to some questions about Natalie Cole. What are the questions?
1. Over 17. (*How many … ?*)
   How many albums has she made?
2. In California. (*Where … for most of her life?*)
3. Twice. (*How many times … ?*)
4. One, a son. (*How many … ?*)
5. Yes, she has. She's won eight Grammies. (*… awards for her singing?*)
6. The University of Massachusetts. (*What university … ?*)
7. For more than 25 years. (*How long … ?*)
8. In 1975. (*When … ?*)

T 7.3 Listen and check.

PRACTICE

Discussing grammar

1 Choose the correct verb form.
1. *(Have you ever been)/ Did you ever go* to a rock concert?
2. I *saw / have seen* The Flash last week.
3. I love rock and roll. I *like / have liked* it all my life.
4. The Flash's concert *was / has been* fantastic.
5. I *have bought / bought* all their albums since then.
6. The Flash *have been / are* together since the early 1990s.

Find someone who ...

2 Choose a number and circle it.

1	2	3	4	5
6	7	8	9	10
11	12	13	14	15
16	17	18	19	20

Now turn to page 122 and match your number to one of the sentences, which begin *Find someone who …* .

Unit 7 • Fame 51

for and since

4 Complete the time expressions with *for* or *since*.

1. _for_ a year
2. _____ half an hour
3. _____ August
4. _____ nine o'clock
5. _____ I was a kid
6. _____ a couple of days
7. _____ months
8. _____ 1999

5 Match a line in **A** and **B** and a sentence in **C**. There is more than one answer!

A	B	C
1. I've known my best friend	from 1994 to 2000.	It's OK. I kind of like it.
2. I last went to a movie	for an hour.	I went camping with some friends.
3. I've had this watch	two weeks ago.	We met when we were ten.
4. We've used this book	since 1989.	I really need a cup of coffee.
5. We lived in our old apartment	since the beginning of the semester.	My dad gave it to me for my birthday.
6. We haven't had a break	for years.	We moved because we needed a bigger place.
7. I last took a vacation	for three years.	It had Tom Cruise in it.
8. This building has been a school	in 1999.	Before that it was an office building.

T 7.4 Listen and check. Make similar sentences about you.

Asking questions

6 Complete the conversation.
What tenses are the three questions?

A Where _____ live, Mi-Young?
B In an apartment near the park.
A How long _____ there?
B For three years.
A And why _____ move?
B We wanted to live in a nicer area.

T 7.5 Listen and check. Practice the conversation with a partner.

7 Make more conversations, using the same tenses.

1. **A** What ... do?	2. **A** ... have a car?	3. **A** ... know Pete Brown?
B I work ...	**B** Yes, I ...	**B** Yes, I ...
A How long ... ?	**A** How long ... ?	**A** How long ... ?
B For ...	**B** Since ...	**B** For ...
A What ... do before that?	**A** How much ... pay for it?	**A** Where ... meet him?
B I worked ...	**B** It was ...	**B** We ...

8 With a partner, ask and answer questions beginning *How long ... ?*

How long have you lived / worked / known / had ... ?

Then get some more information.

Why did you move?   *What did you do before ... ?*   *Where did you meet ... ?*

LISTENING AND SPEAKING
The band Style

1. What kind of music do you like? Who are your favorite bands and singers? If you could meet your favorite band or singer, what would you ask them?

2. **T 7.6** Listen to an interview with two musicians, Suzie and Gary, from the band Style. Put **S** or **G** in Columns 1 and 2. Put ✓ or ✗ in Column 3.

1. What do they do in the band?	2. Who have they played with?	3. Where have they visited?
☐ guitar	☐ UB40	☐ Mexico
☐ keyboards	☐ Britney Spears	☐ Japan
☐ drums	☐ Phil Collins	☐ the UK
☐ harmonica	☐ Genesis	☐ Brazil
☐ vocalist	☐ Ricky Martin	☐ Taiwan
	☐ Bon Jovi	☐ Australia
	☐ Ace	☐ France

Which bands have they played with? Which countries have they been to?

3. Answer the questions.
   1. Why do Suzie and Gary feel tired?
   2. What have they done this year?
   3. Have they had a good time?
   4. What was special about the song "Mean Street"?
   5. How many years have they been together?
   6. Where do they want to go?
   7. What jobs has Gary had?
      What about Suzie? (*She's worked …*)

Language work

4. Make sentences about Suzie and Gary with the phrases in the boxes.

A	B
in April	since 1997
in 1995	about 25
two years ago	15 years
when she got out of college	since he was 17

What tense are the verbs in the sentences from **A**? What about **B**?

5. Ask and answer the questions.
   - What/do/before forming Style?
   - … be/to South America?
   - How/meet each other?
   - How many recordings/make?

Role play

6. Work in groups of four.

   Student A and **Student B** You are members of a band.
   Student C and **Student D** You are are journalists who are going to interview the band.

   Ask and answer questions about:
   - the name of the band
   - what kind of music the band plays
   - who plays what instrument
   - what has influenced their music
   - how long they have been together
   - the records they have made
   - the places they have visited

READING
Celebrity interview

1. Which celebrities are in the news right now? Why are they in the news? What have they done?

2. Look at the article from *Hi! Magazine*. Who is the couple in the interview? Are there magazines like this in your country? What kind of stories do they have?

3. Read the article quickly and put these questions in the right place.

   1. Have there ever been times when you have thought "This relationship isn't working"?
   2. Terry, many professional athletes are tough, but you seem very sensitive. Why is this?
   3. You're both extremely busy in your separate careers. How do you find time to be together?
   4. How did you two meet?
   5. What's it like to be superstars?

4. Read the article again and answer the questions.
   1. Why are they famous?
   2. They are both successful in their careers. What have they done?
   3. In what ways are they normal people? What is not normal about their lives?
   4. How do you know they're in love?
   5. Was it love at first sight?
   6. What is their attitude to newspapers and "other people"?
   7. Why do some people want them to split up?
   8. In what way is Terry unusual for a professional athlete?

5. Work in groups of three. Read the text aloud.

Language work

6. Choose the correct tense.
   1. Donna and Terry *are / have been / were* together for two years.
   2. They *like / have liked / liked* watching TV in the evenings.
   3. They *meet / have met / met* after a baseball game.
   4. They *have lived / live / lived* in their new home since April.
   5. Terry *is / has been / was* in love just once.

Project

7. Buy a magazine like *Hi!*, and find an interview with a famous couple. Bring it to class and tell the class about it.

THE POP STAR AND THE BASEBALL PLAYER

DONNA FLYNN & TERRY WISEMAN

TALK TO *HI! MAGAZINE* ABOUT THEIR LOVE FOR EACH OTHER

This is the most famous couple in America. She is the pop star who has had ten number-one songs—more than any other single artist. He has hit at least 40 home runs every baseball season for the past 4 years and has played on the championship team in the World Series twice. Together they make about $40 million a year. They invited *Hi! Magazine* into their luxurious home.

?

Donna: A lot of the time since we've been together, one of us has been away. We really have to try hard to be together. We have both flown all over the world just to spend a few hours together.
Terry: Obviously, people say, "Oh, you have all this money, what are you going to spend it on?" But the best thing is that money buys us the freedom to be together.

?

Donna: It hasn't changed us. We are still the same people. Newspapers have told terrible stories about us, but it's all lies.
Terry: Our perfect evening is sitting in front of the TV with a pizza. Our favorite shows are *ER* and *Friends*. You won't find photos of us coming out of bars and clubs drunk, after spending the night with a whole load of famous people.

Donna says: "We are so totally in love. Right now, I'm the happiest I've ever been."

?

Donna: I went to one of his games because I liked him and I wanted to meet him. It's funny, because I'm not really interested in baseball, so when I met him after the game, I didn't know what to say to him.
Terry: I'm very shy. We just looked at each other from opposite sides of the room. But I said to my teammate, "She's the one for me. I'm going to marry her someday." Fortunately, she came to another game, and we started talking then.

?

Donna: Not really. Naturally, it's hard when you're away from each other, but in a way this has made us stronger. ▷

54 Unit 7 • Fame

A lot of people would love to see us split up. People have accused Terry of things …
Terry: Of course you have to be ready to give and take in any relationship. There's a trust between us, and as long as that's there, our love will last.

?

Terry: The fact is that this is the first time I've been in love. I think that when you meet the person that you want to spend the rest of your life with, you give your whole life to that person. Nothing else matters.
Donna: We mean the world to each other. Neither of us will do anything to spoil it. **HI!**

Donna and Terry have been together for just over two years. They have lived in their new house since April. She says: "He has good taste —but not as good as mine!"

Terry says: "She's the only woman I've ever loved."

VOCABULARY

Adverbs

1 Many adverbs end in *-ly*.

> slowly   carefully   usually

Find some more examples in the text on pages 54–55.

2 There are also many adverbs that don't end in *-ly*. Find these adverbs in the text.

> together   hard   still   just   of course

3 Complete the sentences with one of these adverbs.

> still
> nearly
> only
> of course
> together

1. "Do you love me?" __Of course__ I do. I'm crazy about you."
2. I called Tom at 10:00 in the morning, but he was _____ in bed.
3. It's our anniversary today. We've been _____ for 15 years.
4. Kate is very fussy about food. She _____ eats pasta and tortilla chips.
5. She was very ill and _____ died, but fortunately she got better.

4 Complete the sentences with one of these adverbs.

> at last   exactly   too   especially   just

1. I like all Russian novelists, __especially__ Tolstoy.
2. "I hate ironing." "Me, _____ . It's so boring."
3. "Are you telling me that we have no money?" "_____ . Not a penny."
4. I met her on December 30, _____ before New Year's.
5. _____ I have finished this exercise. Thank goodness. It was so boring.

Word pairs

1 There are many idiomatic expressions that consist of two words joined by *and*. Here is an example from the text on pages 54–55.

"Of course you have to be ready to **give and take** in any relationship."

2 Match the words.

A	B
ladies	and don'ts
sick	and then
now	and pepper
yes	and quiet
dos	and down
up	and tired
peace	and sound
safe	and gentlemen
salt	and no

3 Complete the sentences with one of the expressions in Exercise 2 above.

1. "Do you still play tennis?" "Not regularly. Just __now and then__ , when I have time."
2. This is a pretty relaxed place to work. There aren't many _____ .
3. Here you are at last! I've been so worried! Thank goodness you've arrived _____ .
4. "Do you like your new job?" "_____ . The money's OK, but I don't like my boss."
5. Sometimes there are too many people in the house. I go out on the patio for some _____ .
6. Good evening, _____ . It gives me great pleasure to talk to you all tonight.
7. "How's your grandmother?" "_____ . There are good days, and then not such good days."
8. It's been so wet! I'm _____ of this rain. When will it ever stop?

T 7.7 Listen and check.

EVERYDAY ENGLISH
Short answers

1 **T 7.8** Listen to the conversations. What's the difference between them? Which sounds more polite?

> 1 When we answer Yes/No questions, we often repeat a subject and the auxiliary verb. Complete these short answers.
>
> | | |
> |---|---|
> | Do you like cooking? | Yes, I _do_ . |
> | Is it raining? | No, it _____ . |
> | Have you been to Hawaii? | Yes, I _____ . |
> | Are you good at chess? | No, I _____ . |
> | Can you speak Spanish? | Yes, I _____ . |
>
> 2 It also helps a conversation if you can add more information.
>
> Do you like cooking?   Yes, I do, as a matter of fact. I especially like Italian food.

2 Complete the short answers. Continue with a line from the speech bubbles below.

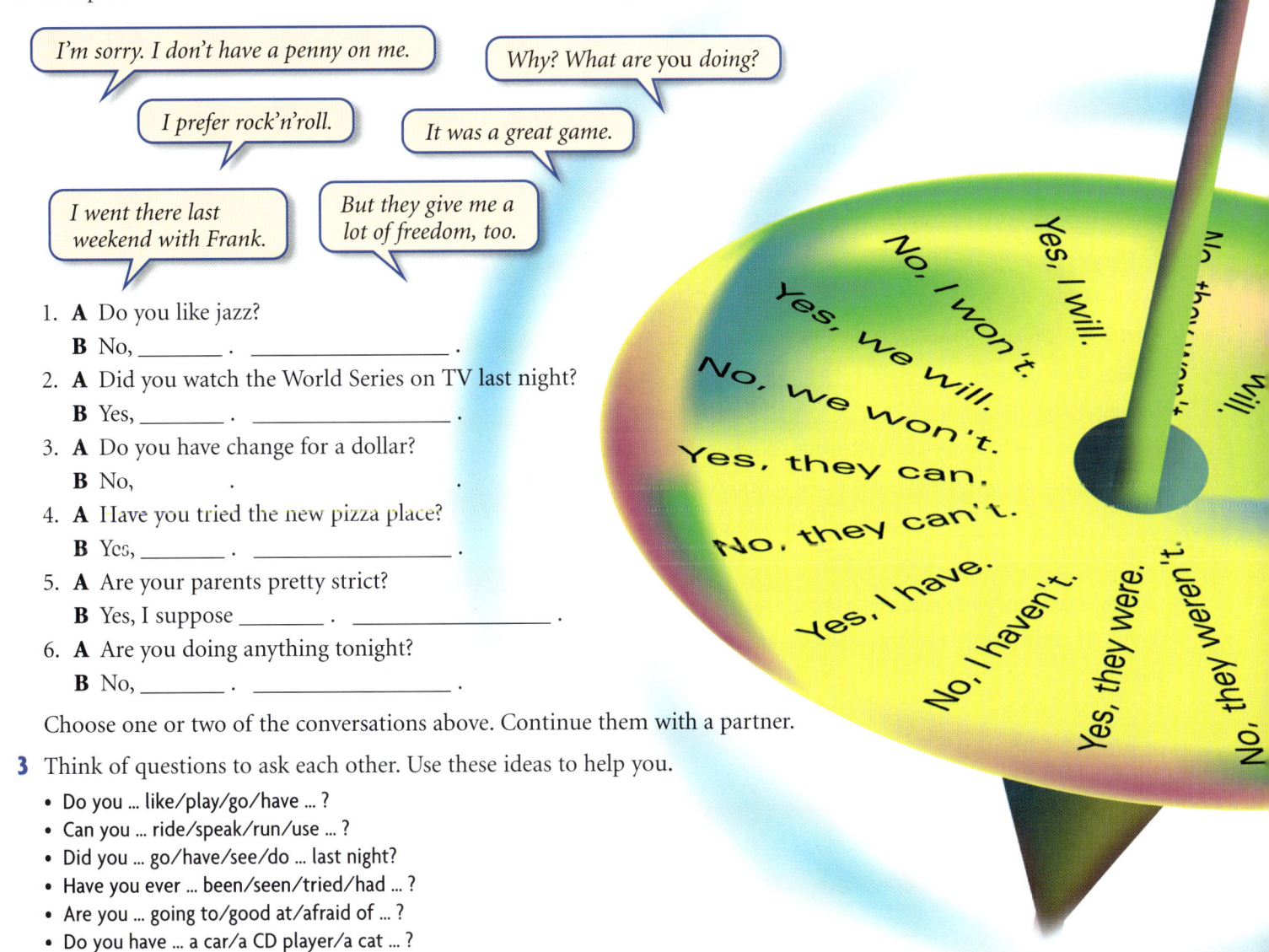

- *I'm sorry. I don't have a penny on me.*
- *Why? What are you doing?*
- *I prefer rock'n'roll.*
- *It was a great game.*
- *I went there last weekend with Frank.*
- *But they give me a lot of freedom, too.*

1. **A** Do you like jazz?
   B No, _____ . _____ .
2. **A** Did you watch the World Series on TV last night?
   B Yes, _____ . _____ .
3. **A** Do you have change for a dollar?
   B No, _____ . _____ .
4. **A** Have you tried the new pizza place?
   B Yes, _____ . _____ .
5. **A** Are your parents pretty strict?
   B Yes, I suppose _____ . _____ .
6. **A** Are you doing anything tonight?
   B No, _____ . _____ .

Choose one or two of the conversations above. Continue them with a partner.

3 Think of questions to ask each other. Use these ideas to help you.
- Do you ... like/play/go/have ... ?
- Can you ... ride/speak/run/use ... ?
- Did you ... go/have/see/do ... last night?
- Have you ever ... been/seen/tried/had ... ?
- Are you ... going to/good at/afraid of ... ?
- Do you have ... a car/a CD player/a cat ... ?

4 Stand up and ask your questions. Use short answers in your replies.

Getting Information

▶ **UNIT 1, page 4**
Student A

PRACTICE
Getting information

Ask and answer questions to complete the information about Judy Dandridge.

Student A When did she start working as a mail carrier?
Student B Twenty years ago, when she was twenty-two.
Why does she drive a truck?
Student A Because she delivers mail long distances to people who live in the country.
What time … ?

Judy Dandridge

Judy Dandridge started working as a mail carrier **20 years ago, when she was 22** (*When?*). She drives a truck because she delivers mail long distances to people who live in the country, far from towns and cities.

She gets up at _____ (*What time?*) and starts work at 5:00. Every day she drives about _____ miles (*How many miles?*). She finishes work at 2:00 in the afternoon.

After work she goes _____ (*Where?*) and has lunch with her husband, Jim. He works _____ (*Where?*). They like gardening, so they often spend the afternoon outside in their garden.

They have two teenage children. Last year Judy, Jim, and the kids went to _____ (*Where?*) and visited Jim's sister. They stayed for _____ (*How long?*).

They're going to Florida next month because _____ (*Why?*). It's Judy's parents' wedding anniversary, and they want everyone to be there.

UNIT 2, page 12
Student A

PRACTICE
Getting information

1 Ask Student B questions about Mike and Nicole to complete your chart.

Name	Town and country	Family	Occupation	Free time/ vacation	Present activity
Mike				• •	
Lucy	London, England	a son and a daughter	part-time teacher	• reading, going to the movies • Florida	drinking tea
Nicole				• •	
Jeff and Wendy	Melbourne, Australia	one daughter and three grandchildren	• He works in an office. • She is a hairdresser	• tennis, swimming • Bali every summer	having a barbecue in the backyard

2 Use your chart to answer Student B's questions about Lucy and Jeff and Wendy.

Getting Information 115

UNIT 1, page 4
Student B

PRACTICE
Getting information

Work together to complete the information about Judy Dandridge.
Ask and answer questions.

Student A When did she start working as a mail carrier?
Student B Twenty years ago, when she was twenty-two.
　　　　　　Why does she drive a truck?
Student A Because she delivers mail long distances to people who live in the country.
　　　　　　What time … ?

Judy Dandridge

　　Judy Dandridge started working as a mail carrier 20 years ago, when she was 22. She drives a truck because <u>she delivers mail long distances to people who live in the country far from town and cities</u> (Why?).

　　She gets up at 3:30 in the morning and starts work at _____ (When?). Every day she drives about 75 miles. She finishes work at _____ (What time?).

　　After work she goes home and has lunch with _____ (Who / with?). He works in a grocery store. They like _____ (What / like doing?), so they often spend the afternoon outside in their garden.

　　They have _____ (How many?) teenage children. Last year Judy, Jim, and the kids went to Los Angeles and visited _____ (Who?). They stayed for ten days.

　　They're going _____ (Where?) next month because their family is having a big party. _____ (Why?)

UNIT 2, page 12
Student B

PRACTICE
Getting information

1 Use your chart to answer Student A's questions about Mike and Nicole.

Name	Town and country	Family	Occupation	Free time/ vacation	Present activity
Mike	Vancouver, British Columbia, Canada	a sister	works for computer company	• skiing, playing ice hockey • Mexico	playing ice hockey
Lucy				• •	
Nicole	Dallas, Texas, the United States	two brothers and a dog!	high school student	• listening to music • Europe	getting ready to go out
Jeff and Wendy				• •	

2 Ask Student A questions about Lucy and Jeff and Wendy to complete your chart.

Getting Information 117

UNIT 1, page 6
Student A

READING
Communication

1. Read the list of messages below. Can you communicate them without using any words? Mime each idea for Student B. He/she must guess what you are trying to communicate.
   - What time is it?
   - Do you want a cup of coffee?
   - I have a headache.
   - I'm hot/cold.
   - I like your haircut.
   - I can't carry this bag.

2. Student B will try to mime some messages. Can you guess what he/she is trying to communicate?

UNIT 3, page 21
Student A

PRACTICE
Getting information

Ask and answer questions to complete the text.

Student A When did Mr. and Mrs. Harman arrive home?
Student B At 10:30 in the evening.
Where was Sue staying?
Student A She was staying with friends.
Why … ?

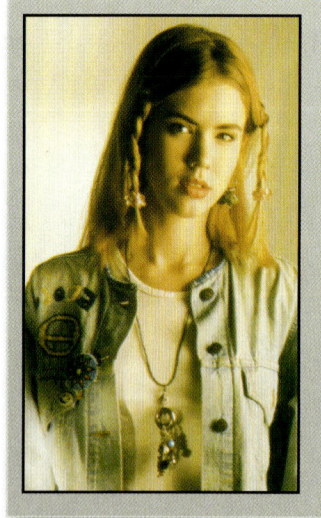

After the party

Mr. and Mrs. Harman arrived home __at 10:30 in the evening__ (When?). Sue was staying with friends. She felt _____ (How?) because her parents would be furious with her.

Her parents started to _____ (What?). Then they phoned Sue and told her _____ (What?).

Sue got back home at 2:00 in the morning. She said _____ (What?), and she promised that she would never have another party.

118 Getting Information

UNIT 6, page 44
Student A

PRACTICE
Comparing four capital cities

1 Read about Washington, D.C., and Tokyo.

WASHINGTON, D.C.	
Founded	1791
Population	606,900
Area	16,863 km2
Temperatures	Jan: 3°C July: 26°C
Rainfall	Jan: 69mm July: 97mm
Km from the sea	150

TOKYO	
Founded	1456
Population	12 million
Area	16,808 km2
Temperatures	Jan: -4°C July: 26°C
Rainfall	Jan: 3mm July: 192mm
Km from the sea	180

2 Ask Student B these questions to find out about Stockholm and Brasilia. Complete the charts below.
- How old is it?
- How big is it?
- How many people live there?
- How hot/cold does it get?
- How wet is it?
- How far is it from the sea?

Student A How old is Stockholm?
Student B It's very old. It was founded in …

STOCKHOLM	
Founded	_____
Population	_____
Area	_____
Temperatures	Jan: _____ July: _____
Rainfall	Jan: _____ July: _____
Km from the sea	_____

BRASILIA	
Founded	_____
Population	_____
Area	_____
Temperatures	Jan: _____ July: _____
Rainfall	Jan: _____ July: _____
Km from the sea	_____

3 Use the information in Exercise 1 to answer Student B's questions about Washington, D.C., and Tokyo.

4 Now compare the four cities.

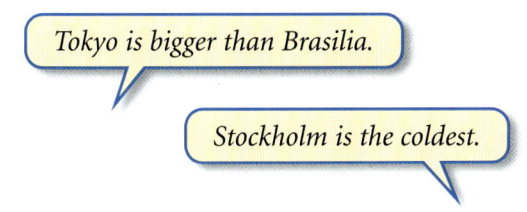

Tokyo is bigger than Brasilia.

Stockholm is the coldest.

5 Compare some cities in your country.

UNIT 1, page 6
Student B

READING
Communication

1. Student A will try to mime some messages. Can you guess what he/she is trying to communicate?

2. Read the list of messages below. Can you communicate them without using any words? Mime each idea for Student A. He/she must guess what you are trying to communicate.
   - I'm tired.
   - Can you swim?
   - Do you have any money?
   - This food is too hot.
   - I'll call you at 7:00.
   - What's that awful smell?

UNIT 3, page 21
Student B

PRACTICE
Getting information

Ask and answer questions to complete the text.

Student A When did Mr. and Mrs. Harman arrive home?
Student B At 10:30 in the evening.
Where was Sue staying?
Student A She was staying with friends.
Why … ?

After the party

Mr. and Mrs. Harman arrived home at 10:30 in the evening. Sue was staying _____with friends_____ (Where?). She felt terrible because _____ (Why?).

Her parents started to clean the house. Then they phoned _____ (Who?) and told her to come home immediately.

Sue got back home at _____ (What time?). She said she was very sorry, and she promised _____ (What?).

120 Getting Information

UNIT 6, page 44
Student B

PRACTICE
Comparing four capital cities

1 Read about Stockholm and Brasilia.

STOCKHOLM	
Founded	1250
Population	692,954
Area	6,488 km2
Temperatures	Jan: -3°C July: 18°C
Rainfall	Jan: 43mm July: 61mm
Km from the sea	0

BRASILIA	
Founded	1960
Population	492,500
Area	5,814 km2
Temperatures	Jan: 20°C July: 19°C
Rainfall	Jan: 94mm July: 46mm
Km from the sea	600

2 Use the information in Exercise 1 to answer Student A's questions about Stockholm and Brasilia.

Student A How old is Stockholm?
Student B It's very old. It was founded in …

3 Ask Student A these questions to find out about Washington, D.C., and Tokyo. Complete the charts below.
- How old is it?
- How big is it?
- How many people live there?
- How hot/cold does it get?
- How wet is it?
- How far is it from the sea?

WASHINGTON, D.C.	
Founded	_____
Population	_____
Area	_____
Temperatures	Jan: _____ July: _____
Rainfall	Jan: _____ July: _____
Km from the sea	_____

TOKYO	
Founded	_____
Population	_____
Area	_____
Temperatures	Jan: _____ July: _____
Rainfall	Jan: _____ July: _____
Km from the sea	_____

4 Now compare the four cities.

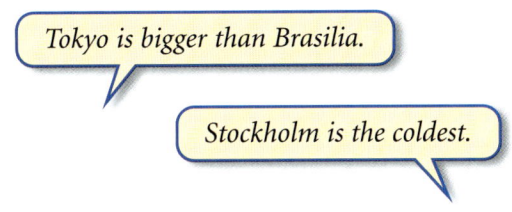

Tokyo is bigger than Brasilia.

Stockholm is the coldest.

5 Compare some cities in your country.

▶ UNIT 7, page 51

PRACTICE
Find someone who...

1. What number did you choose on page 51? Match that number to one of the sentences below.

   1. Find someone who has been to California.
   2. Find someone who has been to Europe.
   3. Find someone who has been to Australia.
   4. Find someone who has written a letter or e-mail in English.
   5. Find someone who has been skiing.
   6. Find someone who has had a party for more than 30 people.
   7. Find someone who has tried Thai food.
   8. Find someone who has flown in a balloon.
   9. Find someone who has been horseback riding.
   10. Find someone who has climbed a mountain.
   11. Find someone who has won a contest.
   12. Find someone who has met a famous person.
   13. Find someone who has read a book by an American or Canadian author.
   14. Find someone who has broken a bone.
   15. Find someone who has been windsurfing.
   16. Find someone who has written a poem.
   17. Find someone who has been in a car accident.
   18. Find someone who has lost something important.
   19. Find someone who has worked on a farm.
   20. Find someone who has **never** failed an exam.

2. Use the information in your sentence to make a question, beginning
   Have you ever ... ?

   > *Have you ever been to California?*

3. Stand up, and ask your classmates your question.
   When someone answers "Yes, I have," ask questions to find out more.

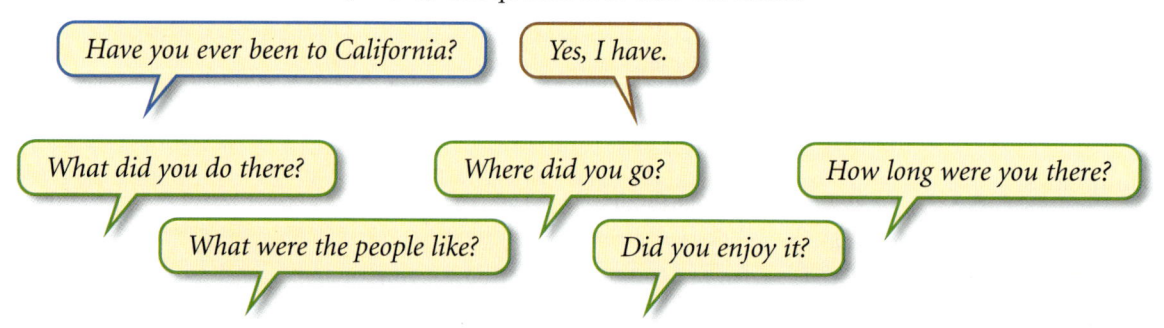

   > *Have you ever been to California?*
   > *Yes, I have.*
   > *What did you do there?*
   > *Where did you go?*
   > *How long were you there?*
   > *What were the people like?*
   > *Did you enjoy it?*

3. Report back to the class.

   > *No one has been to California.*
   > *Paulo and Sonia have been to California. They ...*

Getting Information

Tapescripts

Unit 1

T 1.1 Mauricio

My name's Mauricio Nesta. I come from Brasilia, the capital of Brazil. I'm a student at the University of Brasilia. I'm studying modern languages—English and French. I also know a little Spanish, so I can speak four languages. I'm enjoying the program a lot, but it's really hard work. I started college three years ago.

I live at home with my parents and my sister. My brother went to work in the United States last year.

After I graduate, I'm going to work as a translator. I hope so, anyway.

T 1.2 Carly

Hi. My name's Carly and I come from Toronto, but I live near Boston now with my husband, Dave, and our three children. Dave's an architect. I came to the US 15 years ago when I got married.

I work part-time in a bookstore. I'm also taking courses on the Internet. It's called "virtual university." I study at home, on my computer, and I send my work in by e-mail every week. I'm studying art. It's really interesting and I'm enjoying the program a lot. But it isn't easy having a part-time job and studying, too! Right now, I'm reading about Italian painters in Italian, which is difficult because I speak French quite well but only a little Italian!

I started the program a year ago and it lasts for three years. After I graduate, I'm going to look for a job in an art gallery or museum.

T 1.3

1. I'm reading a good book.
   I booked a room at a hotel.
2. What kind of music do you like?
   My mother is a very kind person.
3. Can you swim?
   I'd like a can of soda, please.
4. What does *architect* mean?
   Don't be mean to your little sister!
5. Please turn on the light.
   This box is very light.
6. Do you want to play tennis?
   We saw a play at the theater.
7. The train's coming.
   Athletes have to train very hard.
8. The phone's ringing.
   What a beautiful ring you're wearing!

T 1.4 Mrs. Snell

I have a new neighbor. He moved in a few weeks ago. I know he has a job, because I see him leaving the house every morning and then coming home in the evening. He's a construction worker, I think. He wears jeans and a T-shirt, so it can't be a very good job. Sometimes he comes home late.

One time he knocked on my door, but I didn't open it. I didn't know who it was, and I don't like to open my door to strangers. So, I've never actually met him and I don't know what I would say to him, anyway. Kids these days. They're so different now!

You know his girlfriend is living with him. I know it's not unusual these days, but I still don't like it, boys and girls living together and not married. It's such a small apartment. I don't know how two people can live there.

He had a party last week. Forty people! The noise! It went on until two in the morning. I didn't sleep all night. He said he was sorry the next day, but it was a little bit late by then.

Oh, there he goes. I can see him now. He's going out with his girlfriend. I wonder what they're doing tonight. Having a good time. Going to a club, probably.

T 1.5 Steve

I moved into this apartment a few weeks ago, and I'm really enjoying living here. There's only one bedroom, and my sister is staying with me right now because she's looking for a job.

I work in advertising. It's hard work, and the hours are really long, but I like it. And it pays well. The office is really casual. No one wears a suit or a tie.

My neighbors are all really nice. I've met them all except Mrs. Snell, I think that's her name. She's very quiet. I never see her or hear her. I knocked on her door once to introduce myself, but she didn't answer. She doesn't like young people or something, I don't know.

I had a party a few days ago. It really wasn't very noisy. About ten of us were here at my place until 11:00 and then we went out to a club. When I saw Mrs. Snell the next day, I said I hoped there wasn't too much noise, but as usual she didn't say anything. She's really odd.

This evening my sister and I are going to visit a friend of ours who's in the hospital, and then we're going out for Chinese food.

T 1.6 Social expressions

1. "How are you?" "Fine, thanks."
2. "Hello, Jane!" "Hi, Peter!"
3. "See you tomorrow!" "Bye! See you then."
4. "Good night!" "Sleep well!"
5. "Good morning!" "Good morning!"
6. "Hello, I'm Elaine Paul." "Nice to meet you, Elaine."
7. "Cheers!" "Cheers!"
8. "Excuse me." "Yes. Can I help you?"
9. "Make yourself at home." "Thank you. That's very nice of you."
10. "Have a good weekend!" "Same to you!"
11. "Thank you very much." "You're welcome."
12. "Bless you!" "Thanks."

Unit 2

T 2.1 Three countries

d. Well, my country's got a population of uhh … about three and a half million, so it's not a big place. Most of the people are from Europe, but about 12 percent are Maori … they were the original inhabitants. A lot of people live in bungalows, which are small houses on one floor, and have a pet. It's a very beautiful country. It's got a lot of mountains, and people love the countryside. Oh, and we're very good at rugby and cricket.

e. My country is the biggest island in Europe, but we have less than 1 percent of the world's population, fewer than 60 million. Most people live in cities and towns, but we've got a beautiful, green countryside, because of all the rain we get. We're famous for drinking tea in the afternoon, and we like to socialize at pubs in the evening, maybe have a pint or two of beer. A favorite hobby is gardening, and our top sports are cricket, rugby, and football—or soccer, as the Americans call it.

f. I come from a big country. It has a lot of wide open spaces. We have a population of … oh … about 280 million. We have big, cosmopolitan cities with people who come from all over the world. But lots of people live in the suburbs and in smaller cities and towns. We're famous for hamburgers and french fries, but we have other kinds of food, too. In fact, you can find almost any kind of food you want here. We like sports—baseball, basketball, and, of course, football!

T 2.2 See p. 12

T 2.3 Questions

Where does he come from?
Is she married?
Do they have any children?
How many brothers and sisters does she have?
What does he do?
What does she do in her free time?
Where do they go on vacation?
What is she doing right now?

T 2.4 Daily life

have breakfast
wash my hair
watch a movie on TV
talk to my friends

take a shower
clean up the mess
do the dishes
have or put posters on the wall

make some coffee
listen to music
relax on the sofa
do my homework

cook a meal
go to the bathroom
put on makeup
read magazines

T 2.5 Home Truths

P = Presenter   C = Carol   M = Mike
D = Dave   A = Alison

P Hello, and welcome to "Home Truths." Today we're going to hear just what couples really think of each other. What drives you crazy about your partner? Here's Carol, talking about her husband, Mike.

C Well, there are a lot of arguments about television in our house. He gets hold of the remote control and then he's always changing channels, so I never see what I want to. All he wants to watch is sports, sports, sports. When I try to talk to him, he doesn't listen because he's watching the TV. And … another thing … he never remembers anything—birthdays, when we're going out, nothing. Oh, and he can't make a decision to save his life. I have to do it all. I decide where we're going on vacation, what car to buy, which restaurant when we go out for dinner … everything.

P So there we have Carol's opinion. What does Mike say about Carol?

M When we're in the car and I'm driving, she constantly tells me how to drive. She'll say "you're going too fast," or "slow down," or give me directions like "make a left turn here," even though I know exactly where I'm going and don't need any help. And then, when I want to watch something on television, like … the news, she always wants to watch a talk show or a movie. And … another thing. She's always on the phone. She spends hours talking to our daughter, and do you know where she lives? Right around the corner.

P But what do they think of their marriage? Here's Carol.

C Well, I can't change him now, so I'll just have to put up with him.

P And Mike?

M We've been married for 25 years, and she's the only woman for me!

P And now we have another couple, Dave and Alison. Oh, and by the way, Dave's an electrician.

A What drives me absolutely crazy is that he starts a job and never finishes it. At work he's so professional, but at home, if I ask him to change a lightbulb in the bedroom, it takes him months. And he's so messy. I tried to train him before we got married, but it didn't work. He just drops things on the floor. I keep saying that I don't want to be his mother as well as his wife. When we go out, he looks so scruffy, even when I'm all dressed up. And his clothes are so old-fashioned. He never throws anything away.

P Oh, boy. Now what does Dave have to say about Alison?

D Well, she's never ready on time. She always finds something to do that makes us late, wherever we go. She's usually doing her hair or putting on her makeup while I'm saying "Come on, honey, it's time to go." And she forgets things. She forgets where she parked the car, she leaves the car keys in the most stupid places. But the most annoying thing about Alison is that she's always right!

P And their final opinions about each other?

A He's great. He's a lot of fun, and he's one in a million.

D See? I told you, she's always right!

P So, there we are. My thanks to Carol and Mike, and Dave and Alison.

T 2.6 Making conversation

J = Jim   M = Maria

1. **J** Hello. What's your name?
   M Maria.
   J I'm … Jim. I'm a teacher. And … where are you from?
   M Rome.
   J Uhh … What … what do you do?
   M I'm a student.
   J Mm. And … how long have you been here in Seattle, Maria?
   M Two months.
   J Are you having a good time?
   M Yes.
   J Can I get you a coffee?
   M No.
   J Do miss your family at all?
   M No.
   J Do you have any brothers or sisters?
   M Yes.
   J Umm … Oh! What do they do?
   M They are students, too.
   J Oh, well, I have a class now. Good-bye, Maria.
   M Ciao.

A = Alice   M = Sergio

2. **A** Hello. What's your name?
   M Sergio. And what's your name?
   A Alice. Where are you from, Sergio?
   M I come from Rio de Janeiro in Brazil, one of the most beautiful places in the whole world. And you, Alice, where do you come from?
   A I come from Canada. What do you do in Rio?
   M I'm an architect.
   A Oh, really?
   M Yeah. I design beautiful buildings for people with lots of money. I'm very expensive.
   A How interesting.
   M And how long have you been a teacher, Alicia?
   A Actually, my name's Alice.
   M I am so sorry. Alicia is the way we say it in Brazil—Alice, I mean.
   A Don't worry. I like the name Alicia. I've been working here for five years.
   M How interesting! Do you enjoy it?
   A Yes, very much. You meet a lot of people from lots of different countries, and I like that very much. Are you enjoying it here?
   M Very, very much. I'm learning a lot of English, I'm making a lot of friends, and even the weather's not so bad! Well, I haven't frozen to death yet, and I've been here for five weeks. Alice, can I get you a coffee?
   A Well, I've got a few minutes before my next class, so that would be nice. Thank you very much …
   M Why don't we …

T 2.7 Everyday conversations

1. What a nice day it is today!
   Yes. It's beautiful, isn't it?
2. How are you today?
   Fine, thanks. How about you?
3. Did you have a nice weekend?
   Yes, we had a great time. We went to the beach and did some shopping.
4. How do you like living in Texas?
   I'm enjoying it. It was kind of strange at first, but I'm getting used to it.
5. Did you have a good flight?
   Yes, no problems. The plane was a little bit late, but it didn't matter.
6. Did you watch the soccer game yesterday?
   No, I missed it. What was the score?
7. What a beautiful coat you're wearing!
   Thank you. I got it in San Francisco last year.

Unit 3

T 3.1   see p. 18

T 3.2   Correct the mistakes

1. Russell woke up at two o'clock.
2. He woke up because he was thirsty.
3. He heard a noise in the kitchen.
4. He found three men.
5. Russell's mother kept her wallet in her bedroom.
6. They left at five o'clock.
7. When they left, Russell watched TV.
8. The police caught the burglars yesterday.

T 3.3   Listen and repeat

a. asked
   showed
   wanted
   walked
   started
b. tried
   carried
c. liked
   believed
   used
d. stopped
   planned

T 3.4   Making connections

1. I broke a cup, but I fixed it with glue.
2. I felt sick, so I went to bed.
3. I made a sandwich because I was hungry.
4. I took a shower and washed my hair.
5. I lost my passport, but then I found it in the back of a drawer.
6. I called the police because I heard a strange noise.
7. I ran out of coffee, so I bought some more.
8. I forgot her birthday, so I said I was sorry.
9. The phone rang, so I answered it.
10. I told a joke but nobody laughed.

T 3.5

Hands up, I've Got a Burger!
Last Tuesday a man armed with just a hot hamburger in a bag stole $1,000 from a bank in Danville, California.
   Police Detective Bill McGinnis said that the robber, who was wearing a mask, entered the Mount Diablo National Bank at about 1:30 P.M. and gave the teller a note demanding $1,000. He claimed that he had a bomb in the bag. The teller said she could smell a distinct odor of hamburger coming from the bag. Even so, she handed the money to the man. As he was running out of the bank, he dropped the bag with the hamburger. He escaped in a car that was waiting for him outside.

Teenage Party Ends in Tears

When Jack and Kelly Harman went away on vacation, they left their teenage daughter alone in the house. Sue, aged 16, wanted to stay at home because she was studying for a test. Her parents said she could have some friends stay over. However, Sue decided to have a party. Everyone was having a good time when suddenly things started to go wrong. Forty uninvited guests arrived, and some of them were carrying knives. They broke furniture, smashed windows, and stole jewelry. When Mr. and Mrs. Harman heard the news, they came home immediately.

T 3.6 A spy story—*The Man with the Golden Gun*

James Bond got back to his hotel room at midnight. The windows were closed and the air conditioner was on. Bond switched it off and opened the windows. His heart was still thumping in his chest. He breathed in the air with relief, then he took a shower and went to bed.

At 3:30 he was dreaming, not very peacefully, about three black-coated men with red eyes and angry white teeth. Suddenly he woke up. He listened. There was a noise. It was coming from the window. Someone was moving behind the curtain. James Bond took his gun from under his pillow, got quietly out of bed, and crept slowly along the wall toward the window. Someone was breathing behind the curtain. Bond pulled it back with one quick movement. Golden hair shone in the moonlight.

"Mary Goodnight!" Bond exclaimed. "What are *you* doing here?"

"Quick, James! Help me in!" Mary whispered urgently.

Bond put down his gun and tried to pull her through the open window. At the last moment the window banged shut with a noise like a gunshot.

"I'm really sorry, James!" Mary Goodnight whispered.

"Shh! Shh!" said Bond. He quickly led her across the room to the bathroom. First he turned on the light, then the shower. They sat down on the side of the bathtub.

"Mary," Bond asked again. "What on earth are you doing here? What's the matter?"

"James, I was so worried. An urgent message came from HQ this evening. A top KGB man, using the name Hendriks, is staying in this hotel. He knows you're here. He's looking for you!"

"I know," said Bond. "Hendriks is here all right. So is a gunman named Scaramanga. Mary, did HQ say if they have a description of me?"

"No, they don't. They just have your name, Secret Agent James Bond."

"Thanks, Mary. Now, I have to get you out of here. Don't worry about me. Just tell HQ that you gave me the message, OK?"

"OK, James." Mary Goodnight stood up and looked into his eyes. "Please be careful, James."

"Sure, sure." Bond turned off the shower and opened the bathroom door. "Now, come on!"

Suddenly a voice came from the darkness of the bedroom. "This is not your lucky day, Mr. Bond. Come here, both of you, and put your hands up!"

Scaramanga walked to the door and turned on the lights. His golden gun was pointing directly at James Bond.

T 3.7 Dates

January eighth, nineteen ninety-eight
July sixteenth, nineteen eighty-five
November twenty-fifth, two thousand two

T 3.8 Dates

the eighth of January, nineteen ninety-eight
January the eighth, nineteen ninety-eight
the sixteenth of July, nineteen eighty-five
July the sixteenth, nineteen eighty-five
the twenty-fifth of November, two thousand and two
November the twenty-fifth, two thousand and two

T 3.9 Dates

June nineteenth
August fifth
July fourth
March first
February third
January twenty-first, nineteen eighty-eight
December second, nineteen ninety-six
April fifth, nineteen eighty
June eleventh, nineteen sixty-five
October eighteenth, two thousand
January thirty-first, two thousand five

Unit 4

T 4.1 see p. 26

T 4.2 see p. 27

T 4.3 *something/someone/somewhere*

1. Did you meet anyone nice at the party?
   Yes. I met someone who knows you!
2. Ouch! There's something in my eye!
   Let me look. No, I can't see anything.
3. Let's go somewhere nice for our vacation.
   But we can't go anywhere that's too expensive.
4. I'm so unhappy. Nobody loves me.
   I know somebody who loves you. Me.
5. I lost my glasses. I looked everywhere, but I couldn't find them.
6. Did you buy anything when you were shopping?
   No, nothing. I didn't have any money.
7. I'm bored. I want something interesting to read, or someone interesting to talk to, or somewhere interesting to go.
8. It was a great party. Everyone loved it.

T 4.4 see p. 29

T 4.5 Buying things

1. A Hello. Can I help you?
   B I'm just looking, thanks.
   …
   B I'm looking for a sweater like this, but in blue. Do you have one?
   A I'll take a look. What size are you?
   B Medium.
   …
   A Here you are.
   B That's great. Can I try it on?
   A Of course. The fitting rooms are over there.
   …
   B I like it.
   A It fits you very well.
   B How much is it?
   A $59.99.
   B OK. I'll take it.
   A How would you like to pay?
   B Cash.
2. A Hi. I wonder if you could help me. I have a bad cold and a sore throat. Can you give me something for it?
   B OK. You can take these twice a day.
   A Thank you. Could I have some tissues too, please?
   B Sure. Anything else?
   A No, that's all. Thanks.
   B OK. That's $8.35.
3. A Could you help me? I'm looking for this month's issue of *Vogue*. Can you tell me where it is?
   B Right there on the middle rack. Next to *Latina*.
   A Thanks.
   B That's $3.50.
4. A Good morning. Can I have a black coffee, please?
   B With sugar?
   A No, thanks. Oh, and a doughnut, please.
   B I'm sorry, but there aren't any left. We have some delicious muffins.
   A I'll have a blueberry muffin.
   B Will that be all today?
   A That's it.
   B That'll be $2.75, please.
   A OK.

T 4.6 Everyday conversations

1. A A book of stamps, please.
   B That'll be six dollars.
2. A How much is this sweater?
   B Twenty-eight fifty.
3. A A loaf of sourdough bread and three rolls, please.
   B That'll be two dollars and eighty-two cents.
4. A Just this book, please.
   B All right. Let's see … . Where's the price? Ah! That's five ninety-five.
5. A How much was your car?
   B Fifteen thousand dollars.
6. A How much was the check for?
   B A hundred and sixty pounds.

Unit 5

T 5.1

Duane
When I grow up, I want to be a basketball player and play for the Los Angeles Lakers, because I want to make a lot of money. After that, I'm going to be an astronaut, and fly in a rocket to Mars and Jupiter. And I'd like all the people in the world and all the animals in the world to be happy.

Maria
I just finished my second year of college, and now I'm going to take a year off. My friend and I are going around the world. We hope to find work as we go. I really want to meet people from all over the world, and see how different people live their lives.

Jim
What I'd really like to do, because I'm crazy about planes and everything about flying, is to have my own business connected with planes, something like a flying school. I'm getting married next June, so I can't do anything about

it yet, but I'm going to start looking this time next year.

Martin
My great passion is writing. I write plays. Two have been performed already, one in Toronto and one in a small, off-Broadway theater in New York. But my secret ambition … and this would be the best thing in my life … I would love to have one of my plays performed on Broadway. That would be fantastic.

Amy
We're thinking of moving, because the kids will be leaving home soon. Meg's 18, she's a high school senior this year, so with any luck, she'll be going off to college next year. And Kate's 15. Jack and I both enjoy walking, and Jack likes fishing, so we're going to move to the country.

Helen
Well, I broke my arm recently, so what I really want to do is to go back to the health club as soon as possible. I really enjoy swimming. At my age, it's important to stay in shape, and I want to be able to travel without feeling sick. I'm going to retire in a couple of years, and I'm looking forward to having more time to do the things I want to do.

T 5.2 Complete the questions

1. A I hope to go to college.
   B What do you want to study?
   A Math.
2. A One of my favorite hobbies is cooking.
   B What do you like to make?
   A Soups, salads, everything.
3. A I get terrible headaches.
   B When did you start getting them?
   A About two years ago.
4. A We're planning our vacation now.
   B Where are you thinking of going?
   A Peru.
5. A I'm tired.
   B What would you like to do tonight?
   A Just stay home and watch TV.

T 5.3 Listen and check

1. A What are the guys doing this afternoon?
   B They're going to watch a baseball game. The Chicago Cubs are playing.
2. A Darn it! I dropped one.
   B I'll pick it up for you.
   A Thank you. That's very nice of you.
3. A What's Sue doing next year?
   B She's going to travel around the world.
   A Lucky her!
4. A The phone's ringing.
   B Oh, I'll answer it. I'm expecting a call.
5. A I don't have any money.
   B Don't worry. I'll lend you some.
   A Thanks. I'll pay you back tomorrow. I won't forget.
6. A What are you and Pete doing tonight?
   B We're going out for dinner. It's my birthday.

T 5.4 Complete the conversation

1. "My bag is so heavy." "Give it to me. …"
2. "I bought some warm boots because …"
3. "Tony's back from vacation." "He is? …"
4. What are you doing tonight?
5. Are you coming to our class party?
6. Congratulations! I hear …
7. I need to mail these letters.
8. Where are you going on your vacation this year?

T 5.5 "You've Got a Friend"

When you're down and troubled
And you need a helping hand
And nothing, but nothing is going right
Close your eyes and think of me
And soon I will be there
To brighten up even your darkest nights.
Chorus
You just call out my name,
and you know wherever I am
I'll come running to see you again.
Winter, spring, summer, or fall
All you have to do is call
And I'll be there, yeah, yeah, yeah,
You've got a friend.

If the sky above you
Turns dark and full of clouds
And that old north wind begins to blow
Keep your head together
And call my name out loud
And soon I'll be knocking on your door.
Hey, ain't it good to know that you've got a friend?
People can be so cold.
They'll hurt you and desert you.
Well, they'll take your soul if you let them.
Oh, yeah, but don't you let them.
(Chorus)

T 5.6 How do you feel?

1. "I feel nervous. I have a test today." "Good luck! Do your best."
2. "I don't feel very well. I think I'm getting the flu." "Why don't you go home and go to bed?"
3. "I'm feeling a lot better, thanks. I have a lot more energy." "That's good. I'm glad to hear it."
4. "I'm really excited. I'm going on vacation to Bangkok tomorrow." "That's great. Have a good time."
5. "I'm sick of this weather. It's so wet and miserable." "I know. We really need some sun."
6. "I'm really tired. I didn't sleep very well last night." "That happens to me sometimes. I just read in bed."
7. "I'm kind of worried. My grandfather's going into the hospital for tests." "I'm sorry to hear that, but I'm sure he'll be all right."
8. "I feel really depressed right now. Nothing's going right in my life." "Cheer up! Things can't be that bad!"

Unit 6

T 6.1 Todd's tennis tour

T = Todd   E = Ellen
E You're so lucky, Todd. You travel all over the world. I never leave Chicago!
T Yeah, but it's hard work. I just practice, practice, practice, and play tennis all the time. I don't get time to see much.
E What about last year? Where did you go? Tell me about it.
T Well … in January I was in Melbourne, for the Australian Open. It's a beautiful city, kind of big and very cosmopolitan, like Chicago. There's a nice mixture of old and new buildings. January's their summer, so it was hot when I was there.
E And what's Dubai like? When were you there?
T In February. We went from Australia to Dubai for the Dubai Tennis Open. *Phew!* Boy, is Dubai hot! Hot, very dry, very modern. Lots of really modern buildings, white buildings. Interesting place, I enjoyed it.
E And Paris?! That's where I want to go! What's Paris like?
T Everything that you imagine! Very beautiful, wonderful old buildings but lots of interesting modern ones, too. And of course very, very romantic, especially in May. Maybe I can take you there sometime.
E Yeah?

T 6.2 What's Chicago like?

T = Todd   F = Todd's friend
F What's the weather like?
T Well, Chicago's called "the windy city" and it really can be windy!
F What are the people like?
T They're very interesting. You meet people from all over the world.
E What are the buildings like?
T A lot of them are very, very tall. The Sears Tower is 110 stories high.
F What are the restaurants like?
T They're very good. You can find food from every country in the world.
F What's the nightlife like?
T Oh, it's wonderful. There's lots to do in Chicago.

T 6.3 Big, Bigger, Biggest!

Melbourne was interesting, but for me, Paris was more interesting than Melbourne, and in some ways Dubai was the most interesting of all because it was so different from any other place I know. It was also the hottest, driest, and most modern. It was hot in Melbourne but not as hot as in Dubai. Dubai was much hotter! Melbourne is much older than Dubai but not as old as Paris. Paris was the oldest city I visited, but it has some great modern buildings, too. It was the most romantic place. I loved it.

T 6.4 see p. 44

T 6.5 see p. 44

T 6.6 Conversations

1. A I moved to a new apartment last week.
   B Really? What's it like?
   A Well, it's bigger than my old one but it isn't as modern and it's farther from work.
2. A I hear Sandy and Al broke up.
   B Yeah. Sandy has a new boyfriend.
   A Really? What's he like?
   B Well, he's much nicer than Al, and much more handsome. Sandy's happier now than she's been for a long time.
3. A We have a new teacher.
   B Really? What's she like?
   A Well, I think she's the best teacher we've ever had. Our old teacher was good, but our new one's even better and she makes us work much harder.

4. **A** Did you get a new car?
   B Well, it's secondhand, but it's new to me.
   A What's it like?
   B Well, it's faster than my old car and more comfortable, but it's more expensive to keep up. I love it!

T 6.7 Living in another country
J = Jane   C = Carla

J When I say that I live in Sweden, everyone always wants to know about the seasons …
C The seasons?
J Yeah … you know how cold it is in winter, what it's like when the days are so short.
C So what *is* it like?
J Well, it *is* cold, very cold in winter, sometimes as cold as -26° Centigrade, and of course when you go out you wrap up in warm clothes, but inside, in the houses, it's always very warm.
C And what about the darkness?
J Well, yeah. Around Christmas time, in December, there's only one hour of daylight …
C One hour!?
J Uh-huh. Only *one* hour of daylight, so you really look forward to the spring. It is kind of depressing sometimes but you know, the summers are amazing. From May to July, in the north of Sweden, the sun never sets—it's still light at midnight. You can walk in the mountains and read a newspaper.
C Oh, yeah. The land of the midnight sun.
J That's right. But it's wonderful, you want to stay up all night, and the Swedes make the most of it. Often they start work earlier in summer and then leave at about two or three in the afternoon, so that they can really enjoy the long summer evenings. They like to work hard but play hard, too. I think a lot of people in the US work longer hours, but I'm not sure it's such a good thing.
C Is it hot in the summer?
J Yeah, it gets pretty warm, but it's not as hot and humid as in some American cities like New York or Washington, D.C. And Swedes don't use air conditioning as much as Americans.
C So what about free time? Weekends? Holidays? Vacations? What do Swedish people like doing?
J Well, every house in Sweden has a sauna …
C *Every* house!?
J Well, every house I've been to. And most people have a country cottage, so people like to leave the city and get back to nature on weekends. These cottages can be fairly primitive—no running water and not even toilets, and …
C No *toilet*?
J Well, *some* don't have toilets but they *all* have a sauna and everyone in the family sits in it together; then they run and jump into the lake to get cool.
C What!? Even in winter?
J Yeah. Swedish people are very healthy.
C Brrr! Or crazy!

T 6.8 Synonyms
1. "Mary's family is very rich." "Well, I knew her *uncle* was very wealthy."
2. "Look at all these new buildings!" "Yes. This city's much more modern than I expected."
3. "Wasn't that movie wonderful?" "Yes, it was great."
4. "George doesn't have much money, but he's so thoughtful." "Yes, he is. He's one of the most generous people I know."
5. "Steve and Elaine's house is huge." "Yes, it's absolutely enormous."
6. "I'm bored with this lesson!" "I know, I'm really sick of it, too!"

T 6.9 Antonyms
1. Mark's apartment isn't very big.
2. Paul and Sue aren't very generous.
3. This TV show isn't very interesting.
4. Their children aren't very polite.
5. John doesn't look very happy.
6. His sister isn't very smart.

T 6.10 Directions
You go down the path, past the pond, over the bridge, and through the gate. Then you go across the road. Take the path through the park and into the woods. When you come out of the woods, just follow the path up the steps and into the museum. It takes about five minutes or less.

Unit 7

T 7.1 Listen and check
1. He sang pop music and jazz. She sings jazz, pop, and rhythm & blues.
2. He recorded more than 600 songs and sold over 50 million records. She has made over 17 albums so far.
3. She was born in Los Angeles and has lived in California for most of her life. He was born in Montgomery, Alabama, grew up in Chicago, then later moved to California.
4. She has been married twice and has one son. She married for the first time in 1976. He was married twice and had five children.

T 7.2 Listen and check
1. Nat King Cole won many awards, including a Grammy Award in 1959 and Capitol Records' "Tower of Achievement" award. Natalie Cole has won eight Grammies and many other awards for her singing.
2. He had his own TV show in 1956 and appeared in a number of movies. She has appeared in several TV specials and TV movies.
3. She received a degree in psychology from the University of Massachusetts in 1972. She has lived mostly in California since then.
4. She has been a recording artist for more than 25 years. She recorded her first album, *Inseparable*, in 1975. With that album she won two Grammy Awards in 1976.
5. Her remarkable album, *Unforgettable with Love*, came out in 1991. On it, she sang the song "Unforgettable" as a "duet" with her father's voice. Since then, the album has sold over five million copies.

T 7.3 What are the questions?
1. How many albums has she made?
2. Where has she lived for most of her life?
3. How many times has she been married?
4. How many children does she have?
5. Has she won any awards for her singing?
6. What university did she go to?
7. How long has she been a recording artist?
8. When did she record her first album?

T 7.4 *for* and *since*
1. I've known my best friend for years. We met when we were ten.
2. I last went to a movie two weeks ago. It had Tom Cruise in it.
3. I've had this watch for three years. My dad gave it to me for my birthday.
4. We've used this book since the beginning of the semester. It's OK. I kind of like it.
5. We lived in our old apartment from 1994 to 2000. We moved because we needed a bigger place.
6. We haven't had a break for an hour. I really need a cup of coffee.
7. I last took a vacation in 1999. I went camping with some friends.
8. This building has been a school since 1989. Before that it was an office building.

T 7.5 Asking questions
A Where do you live, Mi-Young?
B In an apartment near the park.
A How long have you lived there?
B For three years.
A And why did you move?
B We wanted to live in a nicer area.

T 7.6 An interview with Style
I = Interviewer   S = Suzie   G = Gary

I … and that was the latest record from Style called "Give It to Me." And guess who is sitting right next to me in the studio? Suzie Tyler and Gary Holmes, who are the two members of Style. Welcome to the show!
S Thanks a lot. It's nice to be here.
I Now you two have been very busy this year. You've had a new album come out, and you've been on tour. How are you feeling?
S Pretty tired. We've just finished a tour of the UK, and in April we went to Japan, Taiwan, and Australia, so yeah … we've traveled a lot this year.
G But we've made a lot of friends, and we've had some fun.
I Tell us something about your background. What did you do before forming Style?
G Well, we both played with a lot of other bands before teaming up with each other.
I Who have you played with, Suzie?
S Well, over the years I've sung with Lionel Richie and Phil Collins and Bon Jovi.
I And what about you, Gary?
G I've recorded with Genesis and UB40, and I've given concerts with U2. And of course, Ace.
I Why is Ace so important to you?
G Because I had my first hit song with them. The song was called "Mean Street," and it was a hit all over the world … that was in 1995.
I So how long have you two been together as Style?
S Since 1997 … quite a few years. We met at a recording studio while I was doing some work with Bon Jovi. We started talking and Gary asked me if I'd like to work with him, and that's where it all started.
I Suzie, you're obviously the vocalist, but do you play any music yourself?

S Yes, I play keyboards.
I And what about you, Gary?
K I play guitar and harmonica. I can play the drums, but when we're doing a concert we have a back-up group.
I So where have you two traveled to?
S Well, … uhh … sometimes I think we've been everywhere, but we haven't really. We've toured in the UK, and we've been to Japan, Taiwan, and Australia, but we've never been to South America. That's the next place we'd like to go. And then Eastern Europe. I'd love to play in those places.
G You forgot Mexico. We went there two years ago.
S Oh, yeah.
I Over the years you've made a lot of recordings. Do you know exactly how many?
G That's a difficult question, umm …
I Well, about how many?
S Oh, I don't know. Maybe about 25.
G Yeah, something like that.
I And how long have you been in the music business?
G I guess about 15 years. I've never had another job. I've only ever been a musician, since I was 17.
S I've had all kinds of jobs. When I graduated from college, I worked as a waitress, a sales assistant, a painter, a gardener … I could go on and on …
I Well, stop there, because now you're a member of a band. Suzie and Gary, it was great talking to you. Good luck with the new album.
S/G Thanks.
I And now for something different. We're …

T 7.7 Word pairs

1. "Do you still play tennis?" "Not regularly. Just now and then, when I have time."
2. This is a pretty relaxed place to work. There aren't many dos and don'ts.
3. Here you are at last! I've been so worried! Thank goodness you've arrived safe and sound.
4. "Do you like your new job?" "Yes and no. The money's OK, but I don't like my boss."
5. Sometimes there are too many people in the house. I go out on the patio for some peace and quiet.
6. Good evening, ladies and gentlemen. It gives me great pleasure to talk to you all tonight.
7. "How's your grandmother?" "Up and down. There are good days, and then not such good days."
8. It's been so wet! I'm sick and tired of this rain! When will it ever stop?

T 7.8 Short answers

1. A Do you like learning English, Ana?
   B Yes.
   A Do you like learning English, Ana?
   B Yes, I do. I love it. It's the language of Shakespeare.
2. A Are those new jeans you're wearing?
   B No.
   A Are those new jeans you're wearing?
   B No, they aren't. I've had them for ages.
3. A Do you know what time it is?
   B No.
   A Do you know what time it is?
   B No, I don't. I'm sorry.
4. A Can you play any musical instruments?
   B Yes.
   A Can you play any musical instruments?
   B Yes, I can, as a matter of fact. I can play the violin.

Grammar Reference

Unit 1

1.1 Tenses
This unit has examples of the Present Simple and Present Continuous, the Past Simple, and two future forms: *going to* and the Present Continuous for the future.
All these tenses are covered again in later units.
Present tenses   Unit 2
Past tenses   Unit 3
Future forms   Units 5 and 9
The aim in this unit is to review what you know.

Present tenses
    He **lives** with his parents.
    She **speaks** three languages.
    I**'m enjoying** the class.
    They**'re studying** at a university.

Past tense
    He **went** to England last year.
    She **came** to the United States three years ago.

Future forms
    I**'m going to work** as an interpreter.
    What **are** you **doing** tonight?

Form

Verb forms with an auxiliary verb

Affirmative	Question
She is reading.	Is she reading?
They are watching a movie.	What are they watching?
She can drive.	Can she drive?

Verb forms with no auxiliary verb
In the Present Simple and the Past Simple there is no auxiliary verb in the affirmative.
    They **live** in Honolulu.
    He **arrived** yesterday.
Do/does/did is used in the question.
    Do they **live** in Honolulu?
    Where **does** Bill **come** from?
    When **did** he **arrive**?

1.2 Questions

Questions with question words
1. Questions can begin with a question word.

what	where	which	how
who	when	why	whose

    Where's the station?
    Why are you laughing?
    Whose is this coat?
    How does she go to work?
2. *What*, *which*, and *whose* can be followed by a noun.
    What size do you take?
    What kind of music do you like?
    Which coat is yours?
    Whose book is this?
3. *Which* is generally used when there is a limited choice.
    Which is your coat? The black one or the red one?
    This rule is not always true.
    What / **Which** newspaper do you read?
4. *How* can be followed by an adjective or an adverb.
    How big is his new car?
    How fast does it go?
    How can also be followed by *much* or *many*.
    How much is this sandwich?
    How many brothers and sisters do you have?

Questions with no question word
The answer to these questions is *Yes* or *No*.
    Are you hot?   Yes, I am./No, I'm not.
    Is she working?   Yes, she is./No, she isn't.
    Does he smoke?   Yes, he does./No, he doesn't.
    Can you swim?   Yes, I can./No, I can't.

Unit 2

2.1 Present Simple

Form

Affirmative and negative

I / We / You / They	live / don't live	near here.
He / She / It	lives / doesn't live	

Question

Where	do	I / we / you / they	live?
	does	he / she / it	

Short answer

Do you like Peter?	Yes, I do.
Does she speak Thai?	No, she doesn't.

Use

The Present Simple is used to express:
1. a habit.
   I **get up** at 7:30.
   Cindy **smokes** too much.
2. a fact that is always true.
   Vegetarians **don't eat** meat.
   We **come** from Brazil.
3. a fact that is true for a long time.
   I **live** in Miami.
   She **works** in a bank.

2.2 Present Continuous

Form

am/is/are + *-ing* (present participle)

Affirmative and negative

I	'm (am) / 'm not	
He / She / It	's (is) / isn't	working.
We / You / They	're (are) / aren't	

Question

What	am	I	wearing?
	is	he / she / it	
	are	we / you / they	

Short answer

Are you going?	Yes, I am./No, I'm not.	NOT Yes, I'm.
Is Ana working?	Yes, she is./No, she isn't.	Yes, she's.

Use

The Present Continuous is used to express:
1. an activity happening now.
   They**'re playing** soccer in the backyard.
   She can't answer the phone because she**'s washing** her hair.
2. an activity happening around now, but perhaps not at the moment of speaking.
   She**'s studying** math at the university.
   I**'m reading** a good book by Henry James.
3. a planned future arrangement.
   I**'m meeting** Ms. Boyd at ten o'clock tomorrow.
   What **are** you **doing** this evening?

2.3 Present Simple and Present Continuous

1. Look at the wrong sentences, and compare them with the correct sentences.

✗	Hank is coming from Canada.
✓	Hank comes from Canada.
✗	This is a great party. Everyone has a good time.
✓	This is a great party. Everyone is having a good time.
✗	I read a good book right now.
✓	I'm reading a good book right now.

2. There are some verbs that are usually used in the Present Simple only. They express a state, not an activity.

✓	I like soda.
✗	I'm liking soda.

Other verbs like this are *think, agree, understand, love*.

2.4 have/have got

Form

Affirmative

I / We / You / They	have	two sisters.
He / She	has	

Negative

I / We / You / They	don't have	any money.
He / She	doesn't have	

Question

Do	I / we / you / they	have a car?
Does	he / she	

Short answer

Do you have a camera?	Yes, I do./No, I don't.

We can use contractions ('ve and 's) with *have got*, but not with *have*.
   I**'ve got** a sister.
   I **have** a sister.   NOT ~~I've~~ a sister.

Use

1. *Have* and *have got* mean the same. *Have got* is informal. We use it a lot when we speak, but not when we write.
      Have you **got** a dog?
      The prime minister **has** a meeting with the president today.
   In American English, *have + do/does* is much more common.
2. When *have + noun* expresses an activity or a habit, *have* and the *do/does/don't/doesn't* forms are used. *Have got* is not used. Compare these sentences.

✗	I've got breakfast in the morning.
✓	I have breakfast in the morning.
✗	What time have you got lunch?
✓	What time do you have lunch?
✗	He has never got milk in his coffee.
✓	He never has milk in his coffee.

4 In the past tense, the *got* forms are unusual. *Had* with *did* and *didn't* is much more common.
      I **had** a bicycle when I was young.
      My parents **had** a lot of books in the house.
      Did you **have** a nice weekend?
      I **didn't have** any money when I was a student.

Unit 3

3.1 Past Simple

Spelling

1. The normal rule is to add *-ed*.
      work**ed**   start**ed**
   If the verb ends in *-e*, add *-d*.
      live**d**   love**d**
2. If the verb has only one syllable + one vowel + one consonant, double the consonant.
      sto**pp**ed   pla**nn**ed
3. If the verb ends in a consonant + *-y*, change the *-y* to *-ied*.
      stud**ied**   carr**ied**
   There are many common irregular verbs. See the list on p. 153.

Form

The form of the Past Simple is the same for all persons.

Affirmative

I / He/She/It / We / You / They	finished arrived went	yesterday.

Negative
The negative of the Past Simple is formed with *didn't*.
   He walk**ed**.
   He **didn't** walk.

I / He/She/It / We / You / They	didn't (did not)	arrive yesterday.

Question
The question in the Past Simple is formed with *did*.
   She finish**ed**.
   When **did** she finish?

When did	she you they etc.	arrive?

Short answer

Did you go to work yesterday?	Yes, I did.
Did it rain last night?	No, it didn't.

Use

1. The Past Simple expresses a past action that is now finished.
      We **played** tennis last Sunday.
      I **worked** in Tokyo from 1994 to 1999.
      John **left** two minutes ago.
2. Notice the time expressions that are used with the Past Simple.

I did it	last year. last month. five years ago. yesterday morning. in 1985.

3.2 Past Continuous

Form

was/were + *-ing*
(present participle)

Affirmative and negative

I He She It	was wasn't (was not)	working.
We You They	were weren't (were not)	

Question

What	was	I he she it	doing?
	were	we you they	

Short answer

Were you working yesterday?	Yes, I was.
Was she studying when you arrived?	No, she wasn't.

Use

1. The Past Continuous expresses a past activity that has duration.
   I met her while I **was living** in Kyoto.
   You **were making** a lot of noise last night.
   What **were** you **doing**?
2. The activity began *before* the action expressed by the Past Simple.
   She **was making** coffee when we arrived.
   When I phoned Paulo he **was having** dinner.
3. The Past Continuous expresses an activity in progress before, and probably after, a time in the past.
   When I woke up this morning, the sun **was shining**.
   What **were** you **doing** at 8:00 last night?

3.3 Past Simple and Past Continuous

1. The Past Simple expresses past actions as simple facts.
   I **did** my homework last night.
   "What **did** you **do** yesterday evening?" "I **watched** TV."
2. The Past Continuous gives past activities time and duration. The activity can be interrupted.
   "What **were** you **doing** at 8:00?" "I **was watching** TV."
   I **was doing** my homework when Jane arrived.
3. In stories, the Past Continuous can describe the scene. The Past Simple tells the action.
   It **was** a beautiful day. The sun **was shining** and the birds **were singing**, so we **decided** to go for a picnic. We **put** everything in the car …
4. The questions below refer to different time periods. The Past Continuous asks about activities before, and the Past Simple asks about what happened after.

What were you doing What did you do	when it started to rain?	We were playing tennis. We went home.

3.4 Prepositions in time expressions

at	in	no preposition
at six o'clock at midnight at Christmas	in the morning/afternoon/evening in December in the summer in 1995 in two weeks' time	today yesterday tomorrow the day after tomorrow the day before yesterday last night last week two weeks ago next month yesterday evening tomorrow evening this evening tonight
on		
on Saturday on Monday morning on Christmas day on January 18 on the weekend		

Unit 4

4.1 Expressions of quantity

Count and noncount nouns

1. It is important to understand the difference between count and noncount nouns.

Count nouns	Noncount nouns
a cup	water
a girl	sugar
an apple	milk
an egg	music
a kilo	money

We can say *three cups*, *two girls*, *ten kilos*. We can count them. We cannot say ~~two waters~~, ~~three musics~~, ~~one money~~. We cannot count them.

2. Count nouns can be singular or plural.
   This **cup is** full.
   These **cups are** empty.
   Noncount nouns can only be singular.
   The **water is** cold.
   The **weather was** terrible.

much and many

1. We use *much* with noncount nouns in questions and negatives.
   How **much money** do you have?
   There isn't **much milk** left.
2. We use *many* with count nouns in questions and negatives.
   How **many people** were at the party?
   I didn't take **many photos** on vacation.

some and any

1. *Some* is used in affirmative sentences.
   I'd like **some** sugar.
2. *Any* is used in questions and negatives.
   Is there **any** sugar in this coffee?
   Do you have **any** brothers and sisters?
   We don't have **any** dishwashing liquid.
   I didn't buy **any** apples.
3. We use *some* in questions that are requests or offers.
   Can I have **some** cake?
   Would you like **some** soda?
4. The rules are the same for the compounds *someone*, *anything*, *anybody*, *somewhere*, etc.
   I have **something** for you.
   Hello? Is **anybody** here?
   There isn't **anywhere** to go in my town.

a few and a little

1. We use *a few* with count nouns.
   There are **a few eggs** left, but not many.
2. We use *a little* with noncount nouns.
   Can you give me **a little help**?

a lot/lots of

1. We use *a lot/lots of* with both count and noncount nouns.
   There's **a lot of butter**.
   I have **lots of friends**.
2. *A lot/lots of* can be used in questions and negatives.
   Are there **lots of tourists** in your country?
   There isn't **a lot of butter**, but there's enough.

4.2 Articles—a and the

1. The indefinite article *a* or *an* is used with singular, countable nouns to refer to a thing or an idea for the first time.
   We have **a cat** and **a dog**.
   There's **a supermarket** on Adam Street.
2. The definite article *the* is used with singular and plural, countable and noncountable nouns when both the speaker and the listener know the thing or idea already.
   We have a cat and a dog. **The cat** is old, but **the dog** is just a puppy.
   I'm going to **the supermarket**. Do you want anything? (We both know which supermarket.)

Indefinite article

The indefinite article is used:
1. with professions.
   I'm **a teacher**.
   She's **an architect**.
2. with some expressions of quantity.
   a pair of   a little   a couple of   a few
3. in exclamations with *what* + a count noun.
   What a beautiful **day**!
   What a pity!

Definite article

The definite article is used:
1. before oceans, rivers, hotels, theaters, museums, and newspapers.
   the Atlantic   the Metropolitan Museum
   The Washington Times**   **the Ritz
2. if there is only one of something.
   the sun   the president   the government
3. with superlative adjectives.
   He's **the richest man** in the world.
   Jane's **the oldest** in the class.

No article

There is no article:
1. before plural and noncountable nouns when talking about things in general.
   I like potatoes.
   Milk is good for you.
2. before countries, towns, streets, languages, magazines, meals, airports, stations, and mountains.
   I had lunch with John.
   I bought *Cosmopolitan* at South Station.
3. before some places and with some forms of transportation.

   | at home   in/to bed   at/to work   at/to school |
   | by bus   by plane   by car   by train   on foot |

   She goes to work by bus.
   I was at home yesterday evening.
4. in exclamations with *what* + a noncount noun.
   What beautiful **weather**!
   What loud **music**!

Note

In the phrase *go home*, there is no article and no preposition.
I **went home** early.   NOT   ~~I went to home.~~

Unit 5

5.1 Verb patterns 1

Here are four verb patterns. There is a list of verb patterns on p. 153.
1. Verb + *to* + infinitive
   They **want to buy** a new car.
   I'd **like to go** abroad.
2. Verb + *-ing*
   Everyone **loves going** to parties.
   He **finished reading** his book.
3. Verb + *-ing* or + *to* + infinitive with no change in meaning
   It **began to rain/raining**.
   I **continued to work/working** in the library.
4. Verb + preposition + *-ing*
   We**'re thinking of moving**.
   I'm **looking forward to having** more free time.

5.2 *like doing* and *would like to do*

1. *Like doing* and *love doing* express a general enjoyment.
   I **like working** as a teacher. = I am a teacher and I enjoy it.
   I **love dancing**. = This is one of my hobbies.
2. *Would like to do* and *would love to do* express a preference now or at a specific time.
   I**'d like to be** a teacher. = When I grow up, I want to be a teacher.
   Thank you. I**'d love to dance**. = We're at a club. I'm pleased that you asked me.

Question	Short answer
Would you like to dance?	Yes, I would./Yes, I'd love to.
Would you like to come for a walk?	Yes, I would./No, thank you.

Note
No, I wouldn't is not common because it is impolite.

5.3 *will*

Form

will + infinitive without *to*
Will is a modal auxiliary verb. There is an introduction to modal auxiliary verbs on p. 147 of the Grammar Reference. The forms of *will* are the same for all persons.

Affirmative and negative

I	'll (will)	come.
He/She/It	won't	help you.
We/You/They		invite Tom.

Question

When will	he you they	help me?

Short answer

Will you help me?	Yes, I will.

Note
No, I won't is not common because it is impolite. It means "I don't want to help you."
A polite way of saying "no" here is "I'm afraid I can't."

Use

Will is used:
1. to express a future decision or intention made *at* the moment of speaking.
   "It's Jane's birthday." "It is? I**'ll buy** her some flowers."
   I**'ll give** you my phone number.
   "Which do you want? The blue or the red?"
   "I**'ll take** the red, thank you."
2. to express an offer.
   I**'ll carry** your suitcase.
   We**'ll wash** the dishes.

Other uses of *will* are covered in Unit 9.

going to

Form

am/is/are + *going* + *to* + infinitive

Affirmative and negative

I	'm (am) 'm not	going to work.
He She It	's (is) isn't	
We You They	're (are) aren't	

Question

When	am	I	going to arrive?
	is	he she it	
	are	we you they	

Short answer

Are they going to get married?	Yes, they are./No, they aren't.

Use

Going to is used:
1. to express a future decision, intention, or plan made *before* the moment of speaking.
   How long **are** they **going to stay** in Acapulco?
   She **isn't going to have** a birthday party.
   Note
   The Present Continuous can be used in a similar way for a plan or arrangement, particularly with the verbs *go* and *come*.
   She**'s coming** on Friday.
   I**'m going** home early tonight.
2. when we can see or feel now that something is certain to happen in the future.
   Look at those clouds! It**'s going to rain**.
   Watch out! That box **is going to fall**.

***will* or *going to*?**
Look at the use of *will* and *going to* in these sentences.
   I'm **going to make** a chicken casserole for dinner.
   (I decided this morning and bought everything for it.)
   What should I cook for dinner? Umm … I know! I**'ll make** chicken casserole! That's a good idea!
   (I decided at the moment of speaking.)

Unit 6

6.1 What ... like?

Form

what + *to be* + subject + *like*?

| What | 's (is) your teacher
are his parents
was your holiday
were the beaches | like? | She's very patient.
They're very kind.
Wonderful. We swam a lot.
OK, but some were dirty. |

Note

We don't use *like* in the answer.
    She's patient.   NOT ~~She's like patient~~.

Use

What ... like? means "Describe somebody or something. Tell me about them. I don't know anything about them."
Like in this question is a preposition, not a verb:
    "What's Jim **like**?" "He's intelligent and kind, and he's got beautiful brown eyes."
In the following sentences *like* is a verb:
    "What does Jim **like**?" "He **likes** motorcycles and playing tennis."

Note

How's your mother? asks about health. It doesn't ask for a description.
    "How's your mother?" "She's very well, thank you."

6.2 Comparative and superlative adjectives

Form

1. Look at the chart.

		Comparative	Superlative
Short adjectives	cheap small *big	cheaper smaller bigger	cheapest smallest biggest
Adjectives that end in -y	funny early heavy	funnier earlier heavier	funniest earliest heaviest
Adjectives with two syllables or more	careful boring expensive interesting	more careful more buying more expensive more interesting	most careful most boring most expensive most interesting
Irregular adjectives	far good bad	farther better worse	farthest best worst

* Short adjectives with one vowel + one consonant double the consonant: *hot/hotter/hottest, fat/fatter/fattest*.

2. *Than* is often used after a comparative adjective.
    I'm **younger than** Barbara.
    Barbara's **more intelligent than** Sara.
Much can come before the comparative to give emphasis.
    She's **much nicer than** her sister.
    Is Tokyo **much more modern than** New York?
3. *The* is used before superlative adjectives.
    He's **the funniest** student in the class.
    What is **the tallest** building in the world?

Use

1. We use comparatives to compare one thing, person, or action with another.
    She's **taller** than me.
    Tokyo's **more expensive** than Taipei.
2. We use superlatives to compare somebody or something with the whole group.
    She's the **tallest** in the class.
    It's the **most expensive** hotel in the world.
3. *As ... as* shows that something is the same or equal.
    Jim's **as tall as** Peter.
    I'm **as worried as** you are.
4. *Not as/so ... as* shows that something isn't the same or equal.
    She **isn't as tall as** her mother.
    My car **wasn't so expensive as** yours.

Unit 7

7.1 Present Perfect

Form

have/has + -ed (past participle)
The past participle of regular verbs ends in -ed. There are many common irregular verbs. See the list on p. 143.

Affirmative and negative

I We/You/They	've (have) haven't	worked in a factory.
He/She/It	's (has) hasn't	

Question

Have	I we/you/they	been to the United States?
Has	he/she/it	

Short answer

Have you been to Korea? Has she ever written poetry?	Yes, I have./No, I haven't. Yes, she has./No, she hasn't.

Note
We cannot use *I've*, *they've*, *he's*, etc., in short answers.
  Yes, I **have**. NOT ~~Yes, I've~~.
  Yes, we **have**. NOT ~~Yes, we've~~.

Use

1. The Present Perfect looks back from the present into the past, and expresses what has happened before now. The action happened at an indefinite time in the past.
   I've **met** a lot of famous people. (before now)
   She **has won** awards. (in her life)
   She's **written** 20 songs. (up to now)
   The action can continue to the present, and probably into the future.
   She's **lived** here for 20 years. (she still lives here)
2. The Present Perfect expresses an experience as part of someone's life.
   I've **traveled** a lot in Asia.
   They've **lived** all over the world.
   Ever and *never* are common with this use.
   Have you **ever** been in a car crash?
   My mother has **never** flown in a plane.
3. The Present Perfect expresses an action or state which began in the past and continues to the present.
   I've **known** Alicia for six years.
   How long **have** you **worked** as a teacher?
   Note that the time expressions *for* and *since* are common with this use. We use *for* with a period of time, and *since* with a point in time.
   We've lived here **for** two years. (a period of time)
   I've had a beard **since** I left the army. (a point in time)

Note
In many languages, this use is expressed by a present tense. But in English, we say:
   Peter **has been** a teacher for ten years.
   NOT ~~Peter is a teacher for ten years.~~
4. The Present Perfect expresses a past action with results in the present. It is often a recent past action.
   I've **lost** my wallet. (I don't have it now.)
   The taxi's **arrived**. (It's outside the door now.)
   Has the mail carrier **been**? (Are there any letters for me?)
   The adverbs *just*, *already*, and *yet* are common with this use. *Yet* is used in questions and negatives.
   She's **just** had some good news.
   I've **already** had breakfast.
   Has the mail carrier been **yet**?
   It's 11:00 and she hasn't gotten up **yet**.

7.2 Present Perfect and Past Simple

1. Compare the Past Simple and Present Perfect.

   Past Simple
   1. The Past Simple refers to an action that happened at a definite time in the past.
      He **died** in 1882.
      She **got** married when she was 22.
      The action is finished.
      I **lived** in Bangkok for a year (but not now).
   2. Time expressions + the Past Simple

I did it	**in** 1999. last week. two months **ago**. **on** March 22. **for** two years.

   Present Perfect
   1. The Present Perfect refers to an action that happened at an indefinite time in the past.
      She **has won** awards.
      She's **written** 20 songs.
      The action can continue to the present.
      She's **lived** there for 20 years. (and she still does.)
   2. Time expressions + the Present Perfect

I've worked here	**for** 20 years. **since** 1995. **since** I graduated from school.

   We've **never** been to Costa Rica.

2. Compare these sentences.

✗	I've broken my leg last year.
✓	I broke my leg last year.
✗	He works as a musician all his life.
✓	He has worked as a musician all his life.
✗	When have you been to Mexico?
✓	When did you go to Mexico?
✗	How long do you have your car?
✓	How long have you had your car?

Appendix 1

IRREGULAR VERBS

Base form	Past Simple	Past Participle
be	was/were	been
become	became	become
begin	began	begun
break	broke	broken
bring	brought	brought
build	built	built
buy	bought	bought
can	could	been able
catch	caught	caught
choose	chose	chosen
come	came	come
cost	cost	cost
cut	cut	cut
do	did	done
drink	drank	drunk
drive	drove	driven
eat	ate	eaten
fall	fell	fallen
feel	felt	felt
fight	fought	fought
find	found	found
fly	flew	flown
forget	forgot	forgotten
get	got	gotten
give	gave	given
go	went	gone/been
grow	grew	grown
have	had	had
hear	heard	heard
hit	hit	hit
keep	kept	kept
know	knew	known
leave	left	left
lose	lost	lost
make	made	made
meet	met	met
pay	paid	paid
put	put	put
read /rid/	read /rɛd/	read /rɛd/
ride	rode	ridden
run	ran	run
say	said	said
see	saw	seen
sell	sold	sold
send	sent	sent
shut	shut	shut
sing	sang	sung
sit	sat	sat
sleep	slept	slept
speak	spoke	spoken
spend	spent	spent
stand	stood	stood
steal	stole	stolen
swim	swam	swum
take	took	taken
tell	told	told
think	thought	thought
understand	understood	understood
wake	woke	woken
wear	wore	worn
win	won	won
write	wrote	written

Appendix 2

VERB PATTERNS

Verb + -ing	
like	
love	swimming
enjoy	
hate	cooking
finish	
stop	

Note
We often use the verb *go* + *-ing* for sports and activities.
   I **go swimming** every day.
   I **go shopping** on weekends.

Verb + *to* + infinitive	
choose	
decide	
forget	
promise	to go
manage	
need	
help	
hope	
try	to work
want	
would like	
would love	

Verb + *-ing* or *to* + infinitive	
begin	raining/to rain
start	

Verb + sb + infinitive without *to*		
let	somebody	go
make		do

Modal auxiliary verbs	
can	
could	go
will	arrive
would	

Phonetic Symbols

Consonants

1	/p/	as in	**pen**	/pɛn/
2	/b/	as in	**big**	/bɪg/
3	/t/	as in	**tea**	/ti/
4	/d/	as in	**do**	/du/
5	/k/	as in	**cat**	/kæt/
6	/g/	as in	**go**	/goʊ/
7	/f/	as in	**five**	/faɪv/
8	/v/	as in	**very**	/ˈvɛri/
9	/s/	as in	**son**	/sʌn/
10	/z/	as in	**zoo**	/zu/
11	/l/	as in	**live**	/lɪv/
12	/m/	as in	**my**	/maɪ/
13	/n/	as in	**nine**	/naɪn/
14	/h/	as in	**happy**	/hæpi/
15	/r/	as in	**red**	/rɛd/
16	/y/	as in	**yes**	/yɛs/
17	/w/	as in	**want**	/wɑnt/
18	/θ/	as in	**thanks**	/θæŋks/
19	/ð/	as in	**the**	/ðə/
20	/ʃ/	as in	**she**	/ʃi/
21	/ʒ/	as in	**television**	/ˈtɛlɪvɪʒn/
22	/tʃ/	as in	**child**	/tʃaɪld/
23	/dʒ/	as in	**Japan**	/dʒəˈpæn/
24	/ŋ/	as in	**English**	/ˈɪŋglɪʃ/

Vowels

25	/i/	as in	**see**	/si/
26	/ɪ/	as in	**his**	/hɪz/
27	/ɛ/	as in	**ten**	/tɛn/
28	/æ/	as in	**stamp**	/stæmp/
29	/ɑ/	as in	**father**	/ˈfɑðər/
30	/ɔ/	as in	**saw**	/sɔ/
31	/ʊ/	as in	**book**	/bʊk/
32	/u/	as in	**you**	/yu/
33	/ʌ/	as in	**sun**	/sʌn/
34	/ə/	as in	**about**	/əˈbaʊt/
35	/eɪ/	as in	**name**	/neɪm/
36	/aɪ/	as in	**my**	/maɪ/
37	/ɔɪ/	as in	**boy**	/bɔɪ/
38	/aʊ/	as in	**how**	/haʊ/
39	/oʊ/	as in	**go**	/goʊ/
40	/ər/	as in	**bird**	/bərd/
41	/ɪr/	as in	**near**	/nɪr/
42	/ɛr/	as in	**hair**	/hɛr/
43	/ɑr/	as in	**car**	/kɑr/
44	/ɔr/	as in	**more**	/mɔr/
45	/ʊr/	as in	**tour**	/tʊr/